T0271659

THE MAN WHO LOVED SIBERIA

Also by Roy Jacobsen in English translation

The Burnt-out Town of Miracles
Child Wonder
Borders

INGRID BARRØY SERIES
The Unseen
White Shadow
Eyes of the Rigel
Just a Mother

Roy Jacobsen and *Anneliese Pitz*,
from the memoirs of Fritz Dörries

THE MAN
WHO LOVED
SIBERIA

Translated from Norwegian by
Seán Kinsella

MACLEHOSE PRESS
QUERCUS · LONDON

First published in the Norwegian language as *Mannen som elsket sibir*
by Cappelen Damm AS, Oslo, in 2020

First published in Great Britain in 2023 by

MacLehose Press
an imprint of Quercus Editions Ltd
Carmelite House
50 Victoria Embankment
London EC4Y 0DZ

An Hachette UK Company

This translation has been published with the financial support of NORLA

ISBN (HB) 978 1 52941 303 8
ISBN (EBOOK) 978 1 52941 304 5

2 4 6 8 10 9 7 5 3 1

Designed and typeset by CC Book Production
Printed and bound in Great Britain by Clays Ltd, Elcograf S.p.A.

THE MAN WHO LOVED SIBERIA

Foreword

My parents gave me many names, but only ever called me Fritz, and I have never put down my signature as anything else, Fritz Dörries. Being born into a well-known family of entomologists, it was probably only to be expected that I too would develop an overwhelming love of nature. Already at the age of four, the wilds of eastern Siberia cast a spell on me, when my father showed me an illustration of a butterfly with the magical name Parnassius nomion. The drawing had been made by his great exemplar, the entomologist Gotthelf Fischer von Waldheim, a close friend of Humboldt. But the beautiful creature did not exist in any collection, only in that drawing, and in Siberia.

In 1877, at the age of twenty-five, I crossed Japan on foot, after which I sailed to the island of Askold off the coast of eastern Siberia. Then, on the mainland, I mapped the River Suifun in the interior, the areas around the Ussuri and its many tributaries, as well as the even mightier Amur. I roamed the regions east and south of Lake Baikal, along the border with Mongolia, in the Khentii and Yablonovy mountains, and travelled across the Sidimi Peninsula towards Korea through Suchan and Sjantalase.

The names alone make me dizzy.

In my enthusiasm for the venture and the wonders of nature, I defied many dangers, and was privileged to compile large collections of hitherto unknown animals and plants, thousands of tools, weapons and utensils from the indigenous peoples of East Asia, as well as mammals, birds, snakes and lesser species. And, of course, butterflies. All of which museums and institutes bought and placed on display to bring to the attention of the inhabitants of Europe a world virtually unknown to them.

Although still active in my field at the age of ninety, I now, of course, lack the vigour and mettle of the young man who undertook those expeditions. But my many travels have left such profound impressions that both great and small, perilous and innocuous experiences still gleam within my mind's eye. For more than twenty years, the land of Siberia provided me with food, clothing and shelter. I have grown attached to that territory, so much so that to this day I love it more than my own home.

There is nothing more fulfilling than wandering in virgin nature, in the taiga and over the tundra, where winter is harsher, spring more intoxicating, summer more brilliant, and autumn more colourful than any other place on earth. Siberia, to me, is a fairy-tale land.

In many regards, it is also a mythical place, with both a dramatic history and untapped potential. So, despite all the conflicts and tragedies that have been visited upon the land throughout the centuries, I will never lose my faith in it. And I hope the vast riches lying dormant there – be they opportunities for settlement, the wholesome people, or the fertile soil – will render the name Siberia synonymous with the word "future". These are my parting words to my dear daughters.

1

After obtaining the necessary instructions from various institutes in Europe, I was, within the space of eight hectic days, ready to set out on my travels. As mentioned earlier, I was twenty-five years old, with a background as a collector and horticulturist; I had also been a soldier, and the recipient of an extensive private education, particularly in biology, though that being said I am an autodidact, as was my father. And whoever labours under the belief that an insect collector in Siberia is chiefly equipped with a net, a killing jar and a lab coat is greatly mistaken. Shotguns, rifles and other weapons are crucial, and as for clothes, I dressed more or less as the natives did, everything else was useless.

With an advance on my paternal inheritance of one thousand marks, in addition to what I had managed to save up of my horticulturist's wage, it was with no small sense of excitement that I boarded the small steamship *Alwine Said* on February 3, 1877, intending to depart Hamburg the following morning, although the weather that evening was, to put it mildly, terrible.

I settled into the cabin I had been allotted; in order to save money, I had signed up as a galley boy. And seeing no-one else on board, I made my way through the rest of the crew's quarters, where much to my surprise I found only a stoker, so drunk he lay passed out, snoring in a dirty bunk.

I returned to the cabin and went to bed, but had barely fallen asleep when I felt a powerful jolt, whereupon the bow of the ship lifted up and fell down again with a crashing sound. I ran up above and could not believe my eyes: the deck had been transformed into a veritable winter landscape. A howling wind swept the snow through the sea as I groped my way back along the gunwale and discovered that an outbound steamship had smashed into us and destroyed the entire aft deck. Both anchor chains had snapped like string.

Then I finally heard voices. A boat with the first mate and the rest of the crew came through the driving snow, and they rowed alongside and climbed aboard. When they had moored the ship again, we could finally turn in. The following morning Captain Schulz appeared too and asked me to make a report about the incident. And a few days later I had to stand witness in Maritime Court. An English steamship was held responsible for the collision, and only after wasting another two weeks in dock could we depart Hamburg, by which stage it was February 19, so that was quite the start.

On February 21, we found ourselves again having to deal with the weather gods, this time south in the English Channel. Even though we were going at full steam, storm-force winds and heavy seas ensured we made no headway. Captain Schulz, a large man in his prime, with the most impressive Captain Ahab beard, had to stand strapped in on the bridge for over two days. Waves broke constantly across the deck, and anything that was not secured was washed mercilessly into the sea.

A skylight was torn off, and so much water cascaded into the saloon and cabins, one could have taken a bath down there. Fortunately, the pumps functioned properly, and by the time we reached Biscay the sea had finally calmed.

2

We passed the lighthouse at Cape St. Vincent in the far south of Portugal. After a smooth and comfortable voyage across the Mediterranean we reached Port Said, and twenty-fours after that, we had put the Suez Canal behind us.

In the Red Sea we passed the Abdul Kheesan lighthouse opposite the Emerald Mountains and set a course for Aden, where some of the cargo was unloaded. I made small sketches of many of these places, especially the lighthouses, for which I have had a soft spot since boyhood, and because there was little else to do on board other than draw and read. I had brought along all six volumes of *Brehm's Animal Life*, which I had read before but now really immersed myself in as we steamed over the Indian Ocean. An unbearably boring crossing for an impatient young man. The work of galley boy did not take up many hours, and though Captain Schulz was as hard as nails, and liked to subject his people to rough treatment, it was no skin off my nose, I had been a soldier in the German Army.

After passing Ceylon and Singapore we sailed north along the coast of Vietnam and China, eventually anchoring up in Shanghai, where we were met by a sad sight.

These were troubled times in the Middle Kingdom; British, German and French merchants were busy establishing trading houses on the waterfront area, the so-called Bund. They held "concessions" as they were known, and were at odds with the local authorities, who were in turn entangled in civil strife. Currently, the harbour was occupied by hundreds of coolies, the miserable wretches were out of work and condemned to hunger and want. As we docked, the bodies of two children floated between the ship and quay. We learned that the poor creatures had simply passed out from starvation and fallen head first in the river and drowned. No-one had lifted a finger to save them. The authorities had made a small steamer available afterwards to fish them up, which it did before sailing further out and dumping the bodies at a greater depth.

3

In Shanghai I took leave of the *Alwine Said,* bringing all my belongings with me, and went aboard a Japanese steamship. This voyage also passed without problems. The only sighting of land was the island of Iwo Shima, before we anchored up a few days later in Nagasaki, on Kyushu, the southernmost of Japan's large islands. Nagasaki is a beautiful city, built largely by the Dutch and Portuguese, and situated in an even more beautiful bay, surrounded by lush, green hills. It was now April and ahead of me lay spring.

From Nagasaki I sent my trunk on by ship to Yokohama and took lodging at a German hostelry, where I remained for several days to contemplate matters and stock up on provisions. The plan was to go north on foot to Osaka, on assignment for the Botanic Museum in Hamburg, to survey plant life in the country, something no other European had previously done.

However, a peasant uprising had broken out in the region, which the imperial military were doing their utmost to put down. The classical shogunate had come to an end, and the forces that wanted to open Japan up to the outside world were gaining the upper hand; the country had been virtually closed off since 1603.

Fighting in the areas around Nagasaki was especially fierce, and as it was taking place mostly in the valleys, I had to make most of the journey over mountain and hill. There was a strong distrust and dislike of foreigners, and if I were discovered I would doubtless have been accused of spying and faced being shot. Only in the early hours of the morning and at dusk was it possible to sneak down to lower ground and gather the plants for the herbarium that were not to be found in the mountains.

These descents also allowed me opportunity to observe the fighting at close range. But truth be told I could not move about anywhere safely, because the opposing parties climbed increasingly to higher ground in order to wage their battles, the peasants armed with bamboo poles and the soldiers with rifles, leaving no doubt as to who would emerge victorious. I only felt truly safe in the densest bamboo forests, where each evening I built a makeshift shelter of leaves and branches.

4

After roughly two weeks I arrived at the Bungo Strait, a narrow sea channel between Kyushu and the second largest island, Shikoku, which had not been botanised previously either. Over the previous few days, I had heard less of the commotion of war, so I descended from the mountains and began following the shore westwards. By a small village I came upon a fisherman busying himself with some fish traps beside a boat pulled up onto the sand.

He gave a start and stared as though he had seen a ghost – a white European disturbing the tranquillity of the night. Naturally we could not speak to one another, but I showed him my herbaria, as well as a map I had marked in places, and tried with the aid of sign language to explain what I wanted. And I must have made a favourable impression, either that or he was enticed by the money I held out, a small amount I had exchanged into local currency in Nagasaki. In any case he agreed to bring me over the strait. The crossing lasted no more than an hour and took place in the most fantastic moonlight. Already at dawn the next day I could get to work on the task of gathering. Also here on Shikoku I kept to the mountains for safety's sake.

*

With my background in botany and horticulture, I knew where and how to search the terrain, taking light and shade into account, the character of the forest and of other vegetation, soil type, and whether or not water was present. I carried a small manual press, paper, and provisions with me in a bag, working each evening with what I had gathered, sleeping out in the open for the most part and rarely encountering people. Summer temperatures in Japan are mild and pleasant, so I suffered no hardship, and all over I could look down at the famous paddy fields, land as well tended to as the most elaborate gardens in Europe.

After having roamed across the whole of Shikoku, which must have taken about four weeks, I reached the Linschoten Strait, where once again with the help of sign language and a small gratuity, I managed to get a fisherman to ferry me over in the darkness of night to the main island of Honshu.

So, after having walked 580 kilometres, I arrived in the port city of Osaka, where the disturbances did not dominate and I could finally move around relatively freely and try to form an idea of the Japanese way of life, even though I was still unable to speak to anyone. And it was a strange feeling, to be surrounded by such a mass of humanity and not be able to understand a word that was being said. I attracted attention everywhere, gawping and laughter on the part of the men, giggling on the part of the women, and noisy bevies of children tagged along no matter where I went, but I sensed no hostility.

Both women and men wore kimonos, the traditional garment of silk, with colourful and indescribably beautiful embroidery. They clacked around in high wooden clogs, resembling dolls, an unforgettable sight for a European who had only seen drawings of this life. The houses were small, low, made of bamboo, with walls that could be slid open and closed as doors. Several bright temples seemed aloft in the summer-green heights, which here too were planted with rice. I felt transported to an immense theatre, manifold, richly coloured and wondrously strange, not least because everything seemed so well organised.

As a foreigner I was very fortunate to find lodging at an inn, a so-called *ryokan*. I rented a four-mat room, probably at far too high a price. But the innkeeper warmed up as we proceeded in our unsuccessful attempts to understand one another, and by the time I had learned to smile, how to greet somebody, and make sure to remove my shoes every time I crossed a threshold, he demonstrated to me, by use of his arms and legs, how the Japanese bathe, in water so hot one is almost boiled alive.

First one washes oneself thoroughly while sitting naked on a small wooden stool, then one squeezes down into a much too cramped tub, before proceeding to ladle the scalding water over one's head, continuing with this for much longer than is necessary. I realised that not only was the dirt to be removed but the soul also cleansed. The experience of such a bath remains within the body for the rest of the day, as a lingering and reassuring warmth. Subjecting oneself to this torture in wintertime must be even more pleasant.

5

Japan is not only a beautiful land, but particularly striking for a nature lover since it seems as though the towns are built into the terrain, which is then tended to and cultivated as private gardens. The people are small, industrious and appear to have modest needs – rice, millet, fish, herbs and tea providing the most important nourishment. I never saw a meal containing meat nor any sign of cheese or other dairy produce. As time went on, I encountered only friendliness, so it is with fondness I think back on the final stage of my journey in Japan.

It was now mid-June and time was of the essence, so I declared the botanising at an end and caught a train to Yokohama. Along both sides of the railway line lay large stretches of mulberry trees, on which silkworms (*Bombyx mori*) are bred, yielding up to four harvests annually; silk is the country's most important commodity.

The locomotive pulling the little train was like a tiny toy, the carriages were low, with just one step up to the compartment, and the doors and windows were open the entire time. Along the way I also got to see sacred, fire-breathing Fujiyama, which was not erupting at the time but resting beneath a mantle of twinkling white ice.

In Yokohama I lodged at the home of a German merchant, finally meeting someone I could converse with, and only at the sound of my own halting voice did the thought occur to me of how lonesome it had been along the way, and yet this was merely a foretaste of what awaited me.

In Yokohama I once again took possession of the trunk I had sent from Nagasaki, intact and securely locked. It held, amongst other things, weapons, which on no account could go astray. And I could dispatch my first collection to Europe! It was a red-letter day, a collection of plants for the Botanic Museum in Hamburg, with 519 numbered species that I had gathered in the space of the last two months, mainly on Shikoku.

It was made known to me that Yokohama was the largest seaport in the world. I had however seen both Hamburg and Bremen, as well as Antwerp, and took this as an exaggeration, until the following day when I went down to the waterfront and was faced with ships as far as the eye could see, a new world with sail and steam intermingled, along with the traditional Japanese naval, military and civilian vessels, and an enormous fishing fleet, an overwhelming and colourful spectacle.

I had that morning obtained advice from the German Consul and now made my way out to one of the piers, where a Russian steamship was moored up, and a sailor in civilian attire, although armed, was standing guard by the gangway. I started talking to him, in his own tongue, and he was taken aback at first, as Russians usually are when confronted by foreigners with a command of their language. But after only a matter of minutes I was brought up on deck, where the captain stood speaking with a member of the crew. I introduced myself, again in Russian, and he must have detected my accent because he responded in broken German, which was not so odd, as he was Dutch. His name was Hoeck, and he would come to be one of my closest, most trustworthy friends throughout the twenty-two years which lay ahead of me in Siberia.

Hoeck was involved in whaling up north in the Bering Strait, as well as trading in furs with the natives – the Chukchi, Koryak and Ainu peoples. Now, at the close of the winter season, he was on his way home to Russia, where he had his base on the Sidimi peninsula, south of Vladivostok, my intended destination. I would not even need to pay for passage, and already the following day I gathered my equipment, bid farewell to Yokohama and went aboard.

This voyage also passed without any appreciable problems, albeit in constant, exceedingly heavy fog. We sailed between Honshu and Hokkaido without catching the faintest glimpse of those majestic islands. Nevertheless, I remained on the bridge for nearly the entire voyage, spending three strange days chatting with Hoeck, and sailing slowly along as though through a tunnel of grey cotton wool.

6

However, crystal clear sunshine greeted us on our arrival in Vladivostok, and I could finally rest my eyes on the land I had dreamed about since boyhood. It resembled an impenetrable greyish-green mass, not matching my expectations at all, not disappointing as such, just rather nondescript.

I got my baggage ashore and with the help of a letter of recommendation from the consul in Yokohama was able to lodge at the house of a German businessman, Herr Körner, who lived there with a wife and three children. It was not the first time they had welcomed travellers from the homeland. As Germany was lacking in colonies, the state sought to rectify that deficiency by seizing upon every opportunity presented, not least those which arose here in the east with the founding of Vladivostok in 1860. There were a host of other European trading houses in place as well, wooden buildings for the most part, constructed in the Russian style, with the exception of the German chamber of commerce, transported by ship brick by brick halfway around the globe, its imposing structure like a castle in the city.

A diverse number of nationalities were to be found in the winding streets, which were so busy that the many horses could hardly make their way through. A handful of apathetic Russian soldiers tried to maintain order of a kind in this rough society – everyone seemed either to be angry or in a hurry, a great contrast to well-organised Japan. Danish telegraphists, French bakers, Britons, Americans, a veritable Klondike flourishing on this distant shore of the Pacific Ocean; there were brothels, gambling halls and opium dens; on the Peschanyy peninsula a Rhaetian-speaking Swiss was raising deer.

Sixty versts (one verst = 1066.78m) south of the town lay the picturesque island of Askold, a place scientists or researchers had yet to visit; a horseshoe-shaped, extremely lush, volcanic little landmass in the ocean, almost tropical. It was here I hoped to commence my butterfly catch, and not with little expectation, as upon islands separate species and varieties can ofttimes develop; islands are a dream for all naturalists. It was Germany's foremost entomologist, Otto Staudinger – a friend of my father's – who had asked me to visit this very one.

I learned of the existence of a gold wash works on the south of the island and came into contact with the skipper of a schooner acting as a supply boat for the plant. His name was Captain Indwind and he turned out to be a pleasant, affable chap, who without further ado promised me passage on his next trip.

I secured tools, equipment, and food for a month and hired a Manchu named Wanka, whom Herr Körner had put me in touch with. Wanka was about my own age, spoke Russian just as well as Chinese and Manchu, and came from a proud family of hunters that had lived in the region long before the Russians arrived.

We weighed anchor and after a nine-hour crossing made landfall on

Askold on July 15, 1877. The island certainly did not disappoint. The vegetation was more beautiful, richer and more overwhelming than any I had hitherto laid eyes upon, and there was truly something tropical about the island, with a summer temperature like one would experience in Italy.

But there was no civilisation other than the aforesaid gold wash works, so our first order of business was to build a cabin. I located a perfect little shelf of rock on the north of the island, right by a small mountain stream. And Wanka soon proved himself to be both a quick learner and steadfast in purpose. In no more than a week we had a small liveable shelter. This would grow more elegant over time. We even used moments of leisure to fashion broad stone steps at the front, although I do not quite know why. Eventually, from the beach, the building would look almost grand.

7

When a collector arrives in a new area, he turns his attention first and foremost to the vegetation, as most caterpillars live on, and have adapted to, particular trees, bushes and herbaceous plants. Here they feed on the leaves until they pupate and become fully developed butterflies and can endue the landscape with their unique charm. Butterflies are the diamonds of the air, and as they are so closely linked to the vegetation, I will present some of the species on Askold and the mainland below:

Of particular prevalence is the Siberian oak (*Quercus mongolica*), with its broad, bumpy leaves. Then the linden tree (*Tilia mandshurica*) and the elm (*Ulmus campestris*). There is maple (*Acer ukurunduense*), ash (*Fraxinus mandshurica*) and black birch (*Betula dahurica*), whilst white birch only appears sporadically.

In terms of more medium-sized vegetation, there is the Amur cork tree (*Phellodendron amurense*), buckthorn (*Rhamnus frangula*), bird cherry (*Prunus padus*), Siberian Poplar (*Populus suaveolens*) and hawthorn (*Crataegus mandshurica*). I recorded lilac (*Syringa amurensis*) and elder (*Sambucus nigra*), as well as the hazel species Corylus heterophylla, which can form entire bushes.

I observed both Japanese Yew (*Taxus cuspidata*) and the Amur grape (*Vitis amurensis*). Along the streams were alder (*Alnus hirsuta*) and willow (*Salix viminalis*). In clearings in the forest grew nettles (*Urtica dioica*), plantains (*Plantago*), violets (*Viola canina*), knotgrass (*Polygonum aviculare*), dock (*Rumex*), three different species of clover (*Trifolium*), Geraniums (*Geranium vesuvianum*), Speedwell (*Veronica grandis*), dandelions (*Leontodon hostis*), mugwort (*Artemisia vulgaris*) and a locoweed (*Astragalus*) – nature here is, in short, boundlessly luxuriant.

In addition to a large yield of butterflies (Lepidoptera) and beetles (Coleoptera), I discovered an Asarum sibiricum as well as the larvae of the main character himself, Parnassius nomion, the distinctive butterfly in the illustration by von Waldheim that I had seen in childhood and that had enticed me to Siberia, but it was only the larvae, and I was unable to educe mature specimens for want of equipment, something which would not repeat itself.

In low-lying areas of forest, and especially in sunlit clearings with abundant flower growth, I captured a myriad of day-flying butterflies, particularly varieties of the Argynnis, Melitaea, and Lycaenidae species. With heads turned to the sun, the wondrous, shimmering Thecla species – smaragdina, brillantina and diamantina – would sit carefully on oak leaves carefully flapping their delicate wings, before suddenly taking off and circling playfully in the air for a few short moments, only to return to the same leaves, always the same leaves, because under them the remains of the pupae they had emerged from still hung. This aerial circle dance fills the entirety of their short lives, finding a mate, pairing and dying.

In my youth, a friend once asked me what it was I found so fascinating about butterflies, were they not merely fluttering scraps of paper, little more than slightly lifeless confetti? And it occurred to me that I did not have a reasonable answer to give him. I could, of course, have said something about their striking beauty, but that would have been too saccharine. I had the realisation that in addition to the intricate anatomy of the butterfly and the three stages of its development, the metamorphoses, my choice of favourite object had to have something to do with death: a butterfly is quite simply too delicate to be alive. A butterfly is more fragile than any petal, it is a living snowflake. Yet it can still travel thousands of kilometres and withstand the most violent of storms. Butterflies are mysteries, animals which should not exist and yet do, and when one first discovers them, one will never doubt that they are the true soul of the landscape.

One afternoon I showed Wanka a so-called gynandromorph, which forms when an egg does not divide as it should and the specimen develops as half female, half male. The two wings on the right side of the body, for example, are created in the male form, both with regard to range of colour and size, whereas those on the left clearly bear the hallmarks of the female. A gynandromorph is therefore asymmetrical, slightly lopsided and odd, but flies like all other variants and does not appear to have any trouble with the further challenges of existence.

At first, Wanka believed I was pulling his leg, but upon realising that I was serious, he stopped to think for a few moments before breaking into fits of giggles. I enquired as to what was so funny, and he continued to giggle like a juvenile faced with something indecent and asked why on earth our Lord had contrived to create such an abomination. Naturally, I was unable to answer that. He asked if gynandromorphs could produce offspring, and I was unable to give him a clear answer to that either, but I said I would assume not. That settled the issue – Wanka thought me quite mad.

But over the following days he kept returning to the matter, talked more about the gynandromorphs than about all the other specimens we caught, which were for me just as interesting. Could this hermaphroditism befall other animals, he wondered? I told him it could, certain birds, among others, the zebra finch, for example.

"And people?" he asked.

"I don't know." I said.

The entire affair developed into something of a joke between us – gynandromorph, always accompanied by Wanka's embarrassed grin and intricate questions. I derived much pleasure from it, it forced me to think along fresh lines.

8

About once a month we had to travel to Vladivostok to stock up on supplies. While there I also wrote reports and sent some of the material I had collected to Europe, the first sample since the herbarium of Japanese flora. And Herr Körner referred me to a small inn, run by a well-built bear of a man, a bald German with Swiss ancestry. His name was Hans Gammenthaler, and he was loquacious, energetic, had only about half a set of teeth remaining and seemed to think he ran the entire German colony singlehandedly. He was unmarried and childless, drank his own home-brewed beer and schnapps daily, and we became very good friends.

To my astonishment, on one of these trips into Vladivostok, I ran into my younger brother Henry, who was not more than sixteen at the time. But there he was, strolling down the dusty street like it was the most natural thing in the world, dressed as a Russian settler in greyish-brown hessian, worn-out black Cossack boots and a theatrical hat atop his head, which he no doubt hoped would serve to make him look older.

I could not believe my eyes. But Henry was made no different from me, reared in the same spirit, that of our father, and it turned out he had managed to convince the old man to let him follow in my footsteps, without even informing me.

I have no idea how our mother could have gone along with it, but father had secured him a position as an apprentice merchant at the firm of Kunst & Albers, which from a large wooden house in the centre of town sold tools, tea, sugar, American matches, canvas, linen, everything under the sun really, including weapons, ammunition and vodka. Our reunion was both warm and cheerful, and we spent much time together.

Amongst other things, he helped me organise the collections from Askold. He also learned to prepare and write reports after some minor expeditions we made in the regions surrounding the town (although we were warned against venturing into the wilderness; it was full of bandits, so they said, the territory here was as lawless as the one Europeans were at the same time struggling to subjugate in America).

Henry also proved himself a great talent when it came to hunting and collecting, to the extent that he managed to capture no fewer than three specimens of Parnassius, the species I myself had been unable to raise on Askold. I was extremely impressed and incorporated them right away into the collection, which was consequently sent to Europe in his name, to be registered and described by Otto Staudinger.

I spent the winter months largely in the area around Vladivostok, recording, mapping, and hunting, but also getting more acquainted with the people and the language. But in May 1878 I again had to make for Askold, which I was by no means finished exploring. Naturally, Henry wished to accompany me, but he was in my eyes still too young, despite his triumph with the Parnassius, so once again I took Wanka, who was really taking to this life. This time we equipped ourselves for about six months.

It was an abundant spring and even more abundant summer. We carried out a lot of work at night this time. Amongst the many butterflies on the island, I was especially interested in the large green Saturniidae artemis, with its long, elegant tail. It will circle around the collector's head trying in all seriousness to hunt him. Its attacks are fearless and persistent, though never unpleasant, resembling light caresses, to the great misfortune of the butterfly, which thereby makes itself easy prey for the net.

On a honeysuckle (*Lonicera caprifolium*) I came upon the interesting larva of a Melitaea, but as I drew close it suddenly froze, as though in shock, before falling to the ground and lying stiff as a tiny twig. I picked up the larva to study it, and it turned out to be alive and well, which raised the question: had it been playing dead, as a survival strategy, to avoid danger?

And stranger still: I later observed a deer passing the same honeysuckle, and this time the larvae did not react at all. This repeated itself, several times. And neither did they react to birds. So I asked Wanka to approach, and again the larvae stiffened and fell to the ground like twigs. Who would believe it!

Anyone looking at a butterfly wing under a microscope will discover landscapes not found anywhere else, the scales lying in layers upon one another, dusted with glowing specks of colour, like minute, transparent slates on a roof. Then it changes with the light, in small, spectacular flickers, a change in brightness that the human eye can scarcely perceive.

31

It takes a butterfly wing to do this, to teach us quite simply to see, before it is too late. I do not know of a single work of art, be it by Rembrandt or Caravaggio, with that same quality. A butterfly wing is a moment's marvel. There are so many varieties of Luehdorfia alone that one would not think they belonged to the same species, collecting it *alone* could take one lifetime.

There are people who do not believe in God. There are people who have never had a butterfly wing under a microscope, there are people who have never seen a larva play dead, or a swarm of swallowtails fill the shimmering heat of summer with their soundless iridescence. And I do not understand how they can find meaning in life.

9

In eastern Siberia, winter is not a drawn-out death, as it is in Europe. In the space of just a few weeks the leaves change colour completely, before fierce winds suddenly sweep them all to sea, leaving a bleak, pockmarked land behind. Migratory birds now flew above us in great flocks. I had also been commissioned to survey, catch and prepare them by ornithologists Bolau and Novak, whom I had made an arrangement with beforehand; they were at the time amongst Europe's foremost experts. We experienced a few short, intense weeks, until the first snowfall blanketed the island in white.

The presence of deer and pheasant (*Phasianus torquatus*) on the slopes around the dwelling ensured we had no shortage of food. Early winter was spent not only on preparing autumn's yield of specimens but also on catching the winter birds we were still able to get hold of. Wanka increasingly began to resemble a judicious explorer and collector, and was, in fact, fast becoming a great admirer of everything that moved in nature, the many mysteries, he claimed, had previously passed him by.

As mentioned, there was a gold wash works on the south of the island, and we were well acquainted with the custodian there, Herr Yankovsky, a bird lover himself, who frequently contributed useful observations, including a sighting of a rare species of waxwing (*Ampelis phoenicoptera*), which I caught several examples of. It was Yankovsky who – in 1874 – had introduced the pheasants who thrived so well here.

The gold wash works was rather profitable, and apparently a group of bandits on the mainland had got wind of that. They were called the Honghuzi, brutish Chinese thugs who roamed the Russian side of the border, plundering and killing, and then taking refuge on the Chinese side.

One afternoon, Yankovsky came and told me that some fishermen had reported the danger of an impending attack on the island, they had observed the band and heard what they were talking about at first hand. And since our cabin was situated by the only landing site and Yankovsky knew that I had been a soldier, he reasoned it fell to us to defend the island.

We had no dog and would have been in a spot if this band of outlaws turned up while we slept, so even though we were tired after the day's labours – we worked for as long as the light held – we sat night after night with loaded weapons in makeshift hiding places about fifteen paces from one another in anticipation of an attack. For close to three weeks.

On the nineteenth night, we were about to bring the watch to an end, when Wanka whispered over to me that he thought he heard coughing out in the darkness. Shortly after, we heard the sound of oars. As I was reluctant to fire on people, I asked him to yell in Chinese that whoever was out there, ought to turn away immediately, and that we were armed. He shouted at the top of his voice, several times, and by this stage we could discern a grey shape in the darkness. But it continued gliding closer, and when it was some hundred metres away, I fired two shots over their heads.

This too was ignored. Suddenly I saw muzzle flashes and heard bullets ricocheting between the stones around us. There was only one thing to do: I fired what I had towards the boats, reloaded and fired again, while Wanka let loose with buckshot. We heard repeated cries and wails, probably from men wounded, perhaps dying. But then an abrupt silence descended once more, and the black shadow moved slowly but surely out to sea again and disappeared.

We remained at our posts until dawn broke, but even in that light there was nothing to be seen. Had the attack been repelled? We later learned the gang had comprised about thirty men. They made no further advances on the island and were reportedly arrested on the mainland and handed over to the Chinese authorities.

As a reward, Yankovsky presented us ceremoniously with a box of five hundred so-called hunting cigars, of which Wanka was particularly appreciative. He puffed on cigars from morning until night, becoming, I assumed, quite addicted, so when I came home one day and was unable to find my tobacco pouch, I asked if he had seen it.

He looked at me with those shiny onyx eyes of his and, taking it as an accusation of theft, an expression of gross mistrust, was so insulted that he ran out and banged his head until it was bloody against the stone stairway we were building. I had to beg for forgiveness, because of course I found the pouch, where I myself had left it, and several weeks passed before I was back in his good graces, and this was due in no small part to his burgeoning preoccupation with a particular field.

10

My friend had developed an interest in birds, learning astonishingly quickly how to tell the complicated sparrow species apart: the yellow-throated bunting (*Emberiza elegans*), black-faced bunting (*Emberiza spodocephala*), rustic bunting (*Emberiza rustica*), the first migratory birds. The rare chestnut bunting (*Emberiza rutila*), the even rarer Tristram's bunting (*Emberiza tristrami*) as well as the little bunting (*Emberiza pusilla*), of which we secured no fewer than five specimens.

For a time, we had four redpolls (*Carduelis flammea*) living with us in the house, they were on the go from morning until night, chirping and flapping, we gave them oats and water, they flew in and out as they pleased and were a source of great pleasure to us. But one morning we found all four mauled to death by a rat that had found its way in. It was to be the rodent's last misdeed, the following evening Wanka killed it with a well-aimed shotgun round.

He was especially fascinated by eagles, in particular the majestic Steller's sea eagle (*Haliaeetus pelagicus*), which on rare occasions hovered over Askold, and which I would gladly have become more closely acquainted with. But it was the far less shy and more common white-tailed eagle (*Haliaeetus albicilla*) which had grown so accustomed to us that it would swoop down and take the ducks we had shot right from in front of our boots.

On one occasion I rowed around the cliffs on the south of the island in Yankovsky's small boat and managed to shoot three males of the interesting Siberian puffin species (*Fratercula cirrhata*). One was only winged and tried to escape by diving. I was rowing for dear life to get hold of the valuable specimen, when an eagle descended with a sudden mighty splash in front of the boat, re-emerging with the puffin in its claws. I reacted on reflex, firing off two blasts of the shotgun in quick succession, thus securing both specimens. I let Wanka prepare them. This was painstaking work which he was also becoming more skilled in.

Soon after, one of the draught horses from the gold wash works died. I asked Yankovsky if I might have the carcass and had some of his workers drag it up into a narrow gorge. Wanka and I cut some twigs, loosely intertwining them in the existing vegetation over the beast, so that they formed a see-through covering. About twenty-five paces away, we built a little shelter, with a completely closed-off roof, and camouflaged it well. We did not have long to wait.

Mere hours later, ravens (*Corvus japonensis*) had descended on the bait and were well under way with their meal. Shortly after, we also saw the first eagles in the sky, a pair of osprey and a number of white-tailed sea eagles. The osprey (*Pandion haliaetus*) is however extremely shy, and the two of them disappeared. And no Steller's sea eagle to be seen either. But the white tails only grew in number and drew ever closer.

As we crept up to the shelter at dawn the next day, no fewer than seven fine specimens had alighted atop the rotten horse and were eagerly engaged in ripping and tearing at their prey. Wanka wanted to open fire straight away, but I had plans on capturing them alive, and had even sewn some leather hoods to pull over their heads.

Wanka once again thought I had taken leave of my senses, but was soon convinced to go along with it. On the agreed signal, we jumped out and ran as fast as we could towards the bait. The eagles tried to take to the air in panic but remained floundering in the dense network of twigs above them, and after a brief and chaotic struggle we had a hold of two birds each. One of these got away, however, after inflicting some serious bites on Wanka. We received quite a mauling from their claws also, but after some difficulty we got the hoods on them and managed to tie their legs together.

We took them home, set up a perch across the room and placed an anklet on each bird, then fettered them to the perch. Then we removed the hoods. Again, there was a lot of screeching and thrashing, but before long they resigned themselves to their fate. Wanka took on the job of feeding them, with pheasant meat, fish and offcuts, also regularly shovelling out the excrement, of which white-tailed sea eagles produce a lot, and it is pungent. Within the space of a few weeks, they became as much house birds as the redpolls had been, welcoming us home after a day's work, when they expected food and drink. I had all the time I needed to study, describe and paint everything from plumage and anatomy to behaviour, and Wanka named each of them after one of his Manchurian forefathers. They were an old male and two younger females. The females of the species are larger than the males, and the biggest of ours weighed almost six kilos and had a wingspan of 231 centimetres, so it could be quite a squeeze indoors when they all ruffled their feathers at the same time.

At the beginning of April, we gave them their freedom back. But they remained around the house for several days, continuing to welcome us when we arrived home, landing only a metre or two from us, without the slightest fear, and only disappeared when we stopped feeding them, it was a wistful moment for both Wanka and me.

11

Following a turbulent crossing in a rickety Japanese fishing boat, we landed in Vladivostok early in spring. I had scarcely arrived at Gammenthaler's when I bumped into an employee of the German chamber of commerce who excitedly informed me that a tiger was roaming the forests north of the city. The animal had entered a village last night and tried to take a dog. The inhabitants had managed to chase it off but were now terrified of venturing out.

It would have been natural to put together a hunting party, as was usual in such situations, but I had the notion of capturing the tiger alive and asked the fellow to keep quiet about the business for the time being. Now, the literature available about trapping a tiger is slim, to put it mildly, but I had, so to speak, grown up in a zoological garden, and had my father's many practical pieces of advice fresh in mind.

I contacted Henry, who was overjoyed to see me – and equally elated at the prospect of a tiger hunt. We procured in all haste the equipment and tools we considered could be necessary, hired two horses and a wagon and drove the same afternoon up to the village in question. Once there we immediately set to work on the construction of a cage with a vertical trapdoor, which took a little over three days and elicited much mirth amongst the locals, who had no faith in our contraption, but this merely served to spur us on.

We placed iron bars, obtained from a smith in Vladivostok, along one side. At the end of the cage, we made a small space, behind a grille, also with bars, intended to hold a live piglet that could be let in and out through a door at the back of the construction. The bars would prevent the tiger from getting to the piglet. The locals helped us transport the structure to a nearby ravine, where we wedged it between two trees, reinforcing it with some rough lumber, which we assumed could withstand the strength of the wild beast.

We slept another night in the village, and the next morning, as we approached the spot, we could hear the piglet's squeals from fifty paces. I moved cautiously closer and was able to confirm the trapdoor had fallen. We had our quarry. The tiger caught sight of us, hurled itself with all its strength against the iron bars and lamented his lost freedom with a roaring, wide-open mouth. The tiger (*Panthera tigris altaica*) is a so-called "roaring cat" – the larynx is designed to produce this sound.

Eventually, the animal calmed down enough for me to shut the double door in front of the grille. But it continued to roar and scratch at the iron bars and no doubt would dearly have loved to sink its claws into me – and all the others now standing around looking at it with a mixture of fear and delight. I had by then seen many beautiful predators, but not a wild Amur tiger. This full-grown male, of about eight to ten years of age, weighed more than three hundred kilos, and taking its tail into account, was more than four metres long.

We returned the piglet and gave the owner ten roubles for his trouble. With the help of hawsers and a block and tackle we built a hoisting contrivance on the spot and managed to lift the cage and the animal up onto the wagon, which also needed reinforcing. After that we set out for Vladivostok, slowly but surely, and to the persistent sound of growls and roars. It was an interesting journey, taking close to two days with the rickety wagon. We also had to feed and water the tiger along the way. An animal of that size consumes some ten kilos of meat daily, and to that end the locals had furnished us with a deer carcass.

We had ample opportunity to study the play of the muscles beneath the beautiful, doubled fur, the fearsome greyish claws and teeth, as well as the excrement. The tiger has a rippling and menacing mass, not found in any other animal, it is both heavy and agile. In short, majestic.

Approximately halfway to the city it calmed down and began pacing the cage, in figures of eight and tight circles, without emitting any sound. As it can fully retract its claws, and the paws are soft as velvet, there was not a breath to be heard. Thus, we were allowed to experience the silence of the tiger, its chief weapon in the wild, impressive and frightening in equal part. And, truth be told, when one first ventures to look a tiger in the eye, the feeling can be as overwhelming as those stirred when one has a butterfly wing under a microscope.

In the city, word spread like wildfire, both children and adults flocked to admire the beast. Within hours we had an interested buyer, a Russian adventurer, willing to pay 1,800 roubles for the marvel, it truly was a magnificent specimen, and 500 for the cage. He planned to tour Siberia, with the tiger as the main attraction in a travelling circus or zoo. Years later, I heard he had had done very well for himself. As far as I know, this male, whom we named Yascha, lived to be eighteen years of age.

12

After this baptism of fire, I had no choice but to give in to my little brother's incessant nagging. He happily resigned his position at the trading store, without consulting our father, simply blaming this on the poor telegraph connection. And after we had obtained provisions and ammunition, we headed, despite all the warnings, inland and took up residence at an abandoned military post in Baranovsky, by the River Suifun, primarily to collect butterflies and beetles.

After our encounter with Yascha, Henry had become more interested in large predators, and to tell the truth, it was their pelts we would mainly make our living from in the coming years. They fetched a very high price, both here in Asia and in Europe, making us a good deal more money than the scientific objects we collected.

But first spring and summer were at hand.

Between the willow trees along the riverbank, we caught the spring generation of Sericinus telamon var. amurensis Stgr, a beautiful swallow-tail, first discovered and described by us that summer. From a Lonicera edulis – already in leaf – we hammered out approximately forty small Ahlbergia frivaldszkyi larvae. Most butterflies had already emerged from their pupae, and teeming life had broken out, butterflies, wasps, not to mention mosquitos, all destined to make the most of every second of their short lives.

We found several Limenitis helmanni, as well as a new species, later named Limenitis doerriesi, after us. And we captured several Lethe and Parage butterflies, which, we could observe, loved a strange combination of light and shadow: they kept mostly in the shade, preferably sheltering at the bottom of tree trunks, where the warmth of the sun only flickered through. Their sense organs are far more sensitive than ours, and the males compete for these sunspots in the dappled light, which the females also seek out, and thus there exists an interplay, between the sunbeams breaking through and the mating of the animals, that can leave one quite speechless.

One day we were once again sitting captivated by this extraordinary game of light, when the sky suddenly darkened and lightning flashed. Heavy raindrops began to fall, and the miraculous creatures disappeared like dew before the sun, not giving us the slightest opportunity to see where they had got to.

A collector can, however, search for larvae even though it's raining, something which often pays dividends, most importantly when he knows – and he should know – which larvae live on which plants. In addition, the yield of molluscs and slugs is richer on rainy days, as it is with many other rare species one never finds in drier periods.

As soon as the rain ceased and the sun once again shone on the land, we moved through the meadows and edges of forest and caught several specimens of the beautiful Argynnis sagana, Argynnis laodice and Argynnis ruslana, and the astounding, always aloft, never resting Argynnis anadyomene. I must also mention that a stem of ivy gave us almost eighty full-grown larvae of the large, fantastic Ophideres tyrannus amurensis, which eight days later transformed into pupae, and at the beginning of August would emerge as fully developed butterflies.

About one hundred and fifty paces from the military post stood a small log cabin, where a Russian by the name of Andrey Kurtuzov lived along with his wife and two sons aged five and seven; a peasant family living on what the soil gave them, corn, vegetables and potatoes, some hens and a pig. As Kurtuzov was a skilled hunter to boot, the family also had all they could want of meat and fat in the winter months.

One day Kurtuzov had to make the journey to Vladivostok to obtain ammunition and some other equipment, and the plan was for his wife to accompany him to visit a sick relative. Henry and I were going hunting that morning, and prior to that we attended the parents' departure, where the father told the boys it was incumbent upon them to take good care of the dog and the livestock, and was vocal in warning them against all the scoundrels in the area – keep the doors locked day and night.

Addressing the seven-year-old, he said, "but should someone get in, my shotgun is hanging on the wall, and the only thing you need to do is shoot and hit the target, understand?"

The boy had hunted with his father on several occasions, so was not inexperienced when it came to firearms, and he was brave into the bargain. We did think it a touch dramatic, however, since we had not noticed anything in the weeks we had been there. Henry and I then struck out in our separate directions.

Upon returning that evening, I went over to visit the boys, who had made themselves tea and eaten bread with last year's horseradish – everything was tiptop. I sat and chatted with them for a while before going back to the military post.

Henry had arrived home by then too, but he had been tracking a deer and wanted to go out again as soon as we had eaten.

"If I'm not back by ten, I'll spend the night in the forest."

I was tired and went to bed not long afterwards. But I could not have been sleeping very soundly, because I was awakened by a noise in the distance. I realised it was shots that I had heard, three or four at least. My pocket watch showed eleven. I jumped up, dressed and went outside to listen. There was no wind, and I thought I could make out barking, or yelping, coming from the direction of Kurtuzov's house.

Something was obviously afoot, so I sneaked closer, and ten paces from the house I came upon Kurtuzov's dog lying in bloody death throes. I walked the remainder of the way towards the house and called out to the boys – mercifully, they both answered from behind the door. On the steps, however, I stumbled over a man. I reached down to touch him and ascertained that he was warm, bloody but quite dead. I called out anew, the boys recognised my voice and opened up.

"What on earth happened?" I asked.

The eldest boy stood trembling in front of me clutching the shotgun. He turned to his brother, asked him to light the lamp, and said, "we don't need to be frightened anymore."

He pointed to the ceiling, where the intruder had torn off some planks to get down into the room. The boy had done as his father had instructed, immediately grabbing hold of the shotgun and emptying both barrels in the face of the rogue, who had come crashing down.

I stayed the rest of the night with the boys, who both soon fell into a well-deserved sleep. Early the next morning I dragged the body about fifty paces into the forest, dug a makeshift grave, rolled it in and covered it with earth, twigs and grass. There was not enough of his face left to determine if he was Chinese, but judging by his attire, he was a Honghuzi. I buried the dog along with him.

And as a postscript to the drama: the Kurtuzov family moved away shortly afterwards. But some fourteen years later I met the sons again. The eldest, the one who had fired the shots that fateful night, was happily married, and both were living as righteous men in the village of Razdolni, in a house they had built themselves. They were peasant farmers and hunters, in other words typical Russian settlers, but the eldest told me a shudder of fear could still pass through him whenever he thought of that terrible night in Baranovsky, and he could still hear the shots and the sound of the bandit tumbling to the floor.

13

In November the snow laid the landscape under a white shroud, and here I make a conscious association with life's end, because this landscape does not drift peacefully asleep, or go into hibernation, it seems to simply slip into death.

Certain species of winter birds were still to be found though, and we also hunted wolf and fox. We had already killed a number of these and prepared a considerable number of their pelts when a harmless-looking Manchu strolled into the yard one day and inquired as to whether we would be interested in selling them – they were hanging on walls and trees, after all, and were clearly visible from every direction. Naturally we were interested, but he was not willing to meet our price and had to leave empty handed.

One night, about a week later, we were getting ready to turn in when both dogs began barking, and the first thing I thought of was the Honghuzi, that this might have something to do with the Manchu who claimed to want to buy furs, that he had only been here to spy.

I moved quickly to the table to extinguish the candle, but the band were already at the door. They called out, demanding to enter, under the pretext of needing a place to spend the night, they were entitled to it, they claimed, as travellers in need. Henry had a Winchester at the ready and I a revolver.

I let three men in and closed the door behind them. Upon seeing our weapons they immediately wanted to get back outside. I fired two shots over their heads, whereupon one of them spun around and threw a dagger at me. Fortunately, I reacted in time, and the blade missed and stuck in the wall beside me, vibrating. We threatened, jostled and beat them until they were outside again. Oddly, they made no attempt to set fire to the house once they were barred but beat a grumbling retreat back to the woods, our dogs at their heels, barking. And we did not take this as a good sign.

We took turns sleeping, and at the break of dawn we took up pursuit, a simpler matter in the fresh snow. The plan was to confront them in the open, with what weapons we had. We made our way through dense forests and narrow ravines until the late afternoon, when we came to a clearing where the gang had stopped to make food. Judging by the tracks, there were six of them, and three at least were heavily armed, going by the imprints of rifle stocks in the snow. Unfortunately, darkness was falling, so we decided to call off any further pursuit and return home.

Several weeks passed without anything out of the ordinary occurring, and we continued on about our business, hunting foxes and wolves and curing their pelts. But one day I was out alone about five or six versts north of the post, when I came across human footprints that could not have been made by a Russian hunter, not now that Kurtuzov had left the area.

I followed the tracks down into a valley and up the rise on the other side, catching the sound of voices as I neared the ridge. I took out the field glasses and spotted an extremely well-camouflaged cabin, and outside it two Honghuzi were cooking food over a fire. A large number of weapons stood leaning against the wall of the cabin, so I assumed there were more of them, no doubt the same gang who had attempted to raid us a while ago. However, as I was alone, there was little I could do.

A few days later, we had just shot a wild boar (*Sus scrofa*), when fifteen Cossacks, led by a strapping hetman, came riding into the yard. They stated they had orders to track down Honghuzi in the area, part of a gang that had murdered and pillaged their way through a village forty versts further west. Twenty-five of them had been clapped in irons, but some were still at large.

It seemed fortune had smiled upon us. We built a large fire, the Cossacks fortified themselves on our wild boar meat, tea and black bread, and I told the hetman about our experiences, and about the cabin I had observed in the mountains and taken care to mark on the map. He showed an immediate interest and asked to stay overnight, a request we of course granted, the Kurtuzov house was empty now after all. We left early the following morning, on foot owing to the difficult terrain, whilst one of the younger soldiers was sent with the horses in the direction of a road.

After a couple of hours walking we drew close. Not a soul was to be seen and all was quiet, a little snow having fallen during the night. Nor was there any detectable smell of smoke. The hetman divided the troop in two. Each division formed into a semicircle and moved towards the cabin, in a sort of pincer movement. We had not crept more than fifteen or twenty paces when we heard voices. Within a few strides we were by the door.

The eight-man-strong gang were literally caught napping, and had no time to dress or arm themselves, resorting instead to attempting to talk their way out of things when they realised the battle was lost, shouting and screaming in poor Russian that they were innocent subjects of the tsar.

But both the weapons and looted material gave them away, and although they put up resistance, they were no match for the Cossacks.

In no time at all, they had been bound hand and foot and had their plaits cut off, to mark them as criminals. The cabin was burned down, and the weapons, including three Winchesters, were seized. All eight of them were placed in leg irons, and I recognised the man who had thrown the dagger at me amongst them. He sat on the snow, talking nineteen to the dozen, no doubt giving his comrades frantic orders. He received a few heated responses and a row appeared to break out.

The hetman struck the leader – who was bloodied from before – with the butt of a rifle and told him to keep his peace; that served to quieten the rest of them down as well, and we set off.

I asked the hetman what would happen to them now, and he told me he intended to bring them across the frontier to Chifu, whereupon they would be handed over to the Chinese authorities, and in all likelihood face beheading. When I remarked that it could hardly be a pleasant experience to have one's head chopped off with a sword, he told me drily that the Chinese had far harsher punishments than that, they might even chain the prisoners to a large stone or a tree and just leave them there until they starved or froze to death. They would not remove the corpses afterwards either, but leave them there as a deterrent, until wild animals and insects had picked them clean.

After an arduous march of over four hours, we reached the road where the young Cossack was waiting with the horses. We parted ways with the hetman and his troop and made our way back to the military post.

14

There were many wolves, foxes and other predators in the area, owing in no small part to the large deer population. As the military post was located in the middle of the forest, we had frequent visits from wolves. Particularly at night, the hungry beasts would come and devour the offal we left out. In return we were treated to their wonderful howling, which, in the snow-covered wilderness, stirred a singular feeling of pleasure. In the moonlight, with the door ajar, we could observe the entire orchestra standing or sitting on the ground in the glittering snow, some with snouts held high or heads lowered, concentrating fully on making their song as beautiful as possible, especially in January.

That is the time of year the wolves are on heat, and one sees them most often in pairs. Wolves chiefly hunt in a coordinated fashion, tending to follow a common plan. Moving upwind, one wolf will run through a dell while another runs along the crest of the hill. One more will run in the opposite direction, downwind, a companion on its flank, thus chasing their prey towards their fellows. By chance, I came upon four wolves who had hunted down a deer and were in the process of devouring their prey.

I succeeded in taking down a male, but the others got away. My dog immediately took up pursuit, and I hurried after him in the hope of getting more of them in my sights. But two hundred metres further on I found a three-kilo pile of fresh venison in the snow. Shortly thereafter two similar piles. The wolves had emptied the contents of their stomachs in order to run faster. The hunter had to admit defeat.

The Siberian roe deer (*Capreolus pygargus pallas*) was usually everywhere to be seen in Suifun. But with the landscape now frozen stiff, and a lot of snow falling in the mountains, even lying two to three feet deep in the valleys, it made for a very difficult time for the deer, so most of the species stayed put. But one morning, as I was making my way along a wide valley floor I saw a spectacular sight through the field glasses, just a few hundred metres ahead: deer, deer and yet more deer, moving in enormous herds down the side of the valley, several hundred specimens, grey figures gambolling over the dazzling white snow, some grazing, others in motion.

I retreated into a thicket and leaned my rifle against a tree, so with the wind blowing in my direction, I could stand admiring this wondrous sight. It was only when the animals passed that I noticed how fast they were moving. Migration was obviously their main concern, but they also took time to snap at sustenance *while* they ran, presumably because it was necessary to survive. An entire landscape was in fluid, undulating motion, and I counted over four hundred animals. At the front of the herd, an old hind trotted, whilst the older bucks made sure the flanks and the rear were secured. Thus the multitude thrust forward, running, grazing, in large and small leaps through the swirling snow.

I had, of course, no plans to use the rifle. Firing a shot into a herd on the move like this would only have unleashed awful chaos. But one thing makes me indescribably sad: that I was not in procession of a handheld photographic camera at the time. Granted, I did attempt to draw the scene when I returned to the post, but my effort was of course lacking.

Besides Manchurian wapiti (*Cervus canadensis lühdorfi*), the Russians' Isubra, which is not rare even in coastal areas, we found the extremely elegant, somewhat smaller Dybowski deer (*Cervus pseudaxis dybowskii*), which has white patches, and antlers that are highly prized by the Chinese. The Russian hunters were only interested in them in the winter, when the antlers had tines, as the Chinese gladly paid almost two hundred and fifty roubles for those of a five- or six-year-old deer. They ground the soft tines into powder and sold it at very high prices, as it was believed to have curative properties.

But the deer is very shy during the period its antlers grow out, tending to keep to the densest and most impenetrable vegetation.

15

April came. And again the face of the landscape changed. The Suifun flowed ice-free, brown and muddy between mighty banks that slowly but surely became lined in young, green vegetation. The forest floors and meadows burst with new splendour. On trees and bushes the first buds sprouted, thousands of birds withdrew to breeding grounds northwards, creating a bustle in the landscape, day and night we could hear chirping and swishing in the air.

In all my years in Siberia, I have never seen so sweeping a migration as here by the Suifun. Every morning we went out to the marshlands, always in our separate directions and often before dawn. I recognised the cranes (*Grus viridirostris*) by their calls as they flew two hundred metres above me, whilst swans, geese and many types of duck could swoosh so low over the land they threatened to fly straight into me.

Migrating birds of prey also passed through the region. We observed both sea and golden eagles (*Aquila chrysaetos*). The eaglets become adept at flying from an early age, necessitating that the adults cover increasingly larger areas on the hunt for food. We also captured Eurasian sparrow-hawk (*Accipiter nisus*) and besra sparrowhawk (*Accipiter virgatus*), as well as kestrel (*Falco tinnunculus*). And all of these were prepared. We had mastered the art to perfection now. The short-toed snake eagle (*Circaetus gallicus*) had also returned to its territory, and heaven help the snake who ventures out in daylight when a circaetus is on the hunt – a marvellous creature, the circaetus.

In the low forest along the riverbank we also observed many black kite (*Milvus melanotis*), and in the meadows we came across the beautiful black and white striped pied harrier (*Circus melanoleucos*). At night, the owls glided through the wood around us with light wingbeats. Both Eurasian eagle-owls (*Bubo sibiricus*) and Ural owls (*Strix uralensis*) were here as everywhere, to the dread and horror of rodents and smaller species of bird. In the name of science, many of these also fell victim to our deadly lead. On one occasion I came across an eagle-owl (*Bubo bubo*) which had killed a Ural owl (*Strix uralensis*) and was sitting gorging on the carcass in the middle of the open marshland. An owl defeating another owl, two nocturnal species, in broad daylight – nature never ceases to amaze me.

Log

64) Daurian jackdaw (*Corvus dauricus*). Not observed on Askold, but spotted relatively frequently by the Suifun and the Ussuri, one of the first species to return from migration, already in April in flocks of between ten and forty specimens. Their song resembles that of our own jackdaw and can be heard in intense periods morning and evening when they find oats along the roads that have fallen from carts over the winter, their first nourishment in spring terrain. Cautious, shy and difficult to get within range of. Keep preferably to sparse deciduous woodland close to open marshland

and clearings, where as soon as the snow melts they find different types of worms in the moist soil. Nest in small "colonies", four or five pairs together. In one spot we found two uninhabited nests in the same tree. The nests are built in older hollow trees (we never observed otherwise), preferably in old woodpecker holes, and with great variation in distance from the base of the nest cavity to the entrance hole. One nest was just two inches below the hole, so that the brooding female could lie and look out. Another home was three inches deep, and on April 25 we took five eggs from it, all pale, sea green, with tiny, dirty dark grey and light violet speckles. Measurements: . . . On another occasion it proved impossible to reach the bottom of the cavity even though we stretched our arms right down, so we cut a new opening in the tree trunk, taking careful measurements to make sure of the nest's location. Despite the noise of the axe, the brooding bird remained sitting on the eggs. When we finally made it through the trunk, she was completely covered in wood chips. We lifted her out, brushed her off, counted six eggs, measured and described them (see above), made observations and took measurements of her feathers, beak, wings and feet . . . and she remained calm the entire time. We then put her back into place and filled in the new hole with a cut log and some steel wire. She completed the entire incubation period, and five of the six appeared to reach maturity. We made our last observation of them on July 5. For such a shy bird in the crow family, this behaviour is remarkable. The natives (the Goldes) assured us that these birds first appeared about twenty years ago, that is, approximately the same time the first Russian settlers entered the region; what that could mean, I have no idea.

By the Suifun (and later by the Ussuri) there appeared another species of jackdaw which we have still not succeeded in getting hold of. It only appears in very small numbers, as scattered single specimens, both male and female, and exhibits few of the behavioural features of the species of jackdaw described earlier.

65) Azure-winged magpie (*Cyanopica cyana* . . . Pall.) etc.

After a storm lasting three days at the beginning of May, the butterfly collectors' most long-awaited time of year could begin. In river pools and hollows in the meadows there was from day to day an increasing teeming of insect life, and species of frog ending their winter hibernation were to be heard.

We built four wooden cages, covered them with netting, and at the start of July began collecting larvae, which are easier to find than eggs, and have the added advantage of having survived the first phase of development. We placed the larvae in glass jars which we filled with feed, mainly leaves and herbs, but also a little sugar and honey, since the available berries were not ripe.

To avoid strong sunlight, all of this was carried out indoors, which also meant we could be assured of raising specimens free from parasites. After about four weeks, the larvae had grown many times their size and become pupae, which we then picked from the jars and hung up in the cages, where, after two to three weeks, they transformed into miracles, there is no other word for it.

At its most intense, the gentle clacking sounded like music to our ears from morning to night, and was always combined with great excitement, as we were familiar with almost all the species and were naturally excited about what might reveal itself – a new discovery?

*

Of course, this "laboratory work" cannot compensate for capturing the larvae in nature, where they are both difficult to locate and to identify. That is dependent on experience, and we were getting ever more of it.

We were also making rich nocturnal discoveries. On a bracken-covered island in the river I lay in wait for three nights on the hunt for a small summer butterfly, a so-called micro. And a total of nine hundred specimens would in the course of this spring and summer be recorded – 145 different species – which must be seen as a dramatic success, taking into consideration the fact that many had not previously been registered. I might also point out that it can often be quite a feat – usually under-taken amid intense swarms of midges and mosquitoes! – to pierce the tiny micro undamaged with a needle; it measures no more than five or six millimetres, and unlike the larger species, is meant to stand with outspread wings, also in collection boxes.

The two species of bear found here, the brown bear (*Ursus arctos*) and the Asian black bear (*Ursus thibetanus*), had left their dens long ago, but kept chiefly to the mountains, where the cones of the Swiss pine (*Pinus cembra*) cover the forest floor and offer both them and the wild boar all the nourishment they could wish for. In the river, the otter (*Lutra vulgaris*) once again appeared, that feisty mustelid who throughout the winter had endured a hard existence by small open springs in the moun-tains. On the riverbanks, the Siberian weasel (*Mustela sibirica*) hunted, and in the forests the squirrel frolicked, while the forest floor belonged to the Siberian chipmunk (*Eutamias sibiricus*), a beautiful yellow and black striped rodent which feeds on both birds and eggs.

16

As summer neared an end, we packed up, left our wretched yet beloved abode, and took our treasures to Vladivostok, where we spent almost three weeks organising and cataloguing our finds: the thirty-six species of bird were sent in their entirety to Dr Bolau at the Natural History Museum in Hamburg. Most of the nearly a thousand butterflies went once again – via father – to Otto Staudinger, whilst the cured hides – beasts of prey, rodents and others – were dispatched to various institutes in Europe where father had contacts. We also sold a good many pelts at the market in town in order to finance the next expedition.

We had received by telegraph new commissions and what we required of letters of recommendation, and in addition had got hold of some copies of Prince Kropotkin's 1875 map of East Siberia, unquestionably the best in existence. So we followed the main road north to the bank of the Ussuri, the single mighty river serving as a natural border between China and Russia. There, we went aboard a steamboat that brought us downriver to its confluence with the Amur at Kazakevichevo, a settlement at the foot of the Khekhtsir hills, where we wanted to focus primarily on autumn and winter birds.

We had once again been granted permission to set up our head-quarters at an abandoned military post, and we mapped what we could of the area in the two months we had available before winter set in. At the beginning of December, we packed all our equipment and set out with dogs and sleigh to hunt for furs on land we had in mind east of the Ussuri.

As the ice on the river now held, we could head up the Ussuri, and thereafter into a tributary, the Khor. For three nights running we spent the night in a tent in thirty-eight degrees below zero. We saw few tracks, but continued further up, eventually having to drive along the bank, as the ice grew more unsafe the higher we went, and the current became swifter.

One morning, we spotted a sea eagle sitting a hundred metres off, devouring a salmon it had taken in the open water. We calmed the dogs, and I walked onto the ice to take a closer look at the bird; this was a reunion with an old friend. It was the species Wanka and I had shared a house with for several months on Askold. But not more than ten short paces from the perfect specimen – it was a huge female – one of my legs went through the ice, and then the other. Only with a frantic, strenuous effort did I manage to get back up before the current pulled me under, and crawl back far enough for Henry to throw me a rope and pull me to the bank. He got a fire going while I struggled to take off my clothes, which were already rigid with ice, then rushed to get some dry things on, and tried to recover by hopping up and down and swinging my arms. Despite all the ruckus, the eagle did not even offer us a glance, just calmly finished feeding, took to the air and flew in idle majesty further into the valley. Neither of us considered firing a shot, as is only proper on encountering a friend.

On the seventh day we finally came across tracks, those of a fox, a wolf and a brown-eared pheasant (*Crossoptilon mantchuricum*). And in temperatures of nearly forty below zero we erected the tent in the shelter of a dense clump of bushes and used the short amount of daylight to gather wood for three weeks. Then at intervals of about one hundred metres along the riverbank, we laid out poison pills packed into lumps of unsalted butter, to avoid gunshot wounds to the animals.

We know from fables that the fox is a cunning and shrewd creature, and in this case we really had a disobliging specimen to deal with. Although attracted to the butter, it carried out all manner of strange manoeuvres around the bait: sneaking up to the lump, jumping to one side, before approaching anew and flicking a paw at it to send it flying; movements we could tell from the imprints in the snow. It resembled a closely choreographed dance.

I let the lump of butter lie, returned the following day and observed that it had again changed position. I followed the tracks and saw that the fox had crossed the river, somehow managing to get through the freezing water. I left the bait where it was, and on my third visit I was able to ascertain that Reynard had been there once again, but now only to spray the lump of butter with urine, and after that I gave up.

The wolf, on the other hand, had not seemed to bother with any inspection whatsoever. It went straight for the bait, gobbled up both butter and pills and now lay dead just a few feet away. We took as many specimens as we had room for on the sleigh. The carcasses would have to lie indoors to thaw out before we could prepare them, so we stored them in another tent for the time being.

We also shot what we needed of foxes and pheasants, both for food and for the collection, and after three weeks we returned with the fruits of our labour to our headquarters in Kazakevichevo. There we rested a few days, thawed out the carcasses, skinned them and cured the pelts. It was our job to remove everything that could rot, and thereafter dry and pack the pelts with as much care as possible. The actual stuffing and mounting took place in the museums in Europe.

17

We had been also assigned by the Museum of Ethnology in Hamburg to study the many indigenous peoples in East Siberia. And the region we now found ourselves in was home to the Goldes, the people I made brief mention of previously, who apprised us of that other species of jackdaw's migratory routes.

The Goldes reside mainly in mud cabins along the length of the Ussuri and its many tributaries. They subsisted on fishing and hunting, and although well acquainted with firearms, they still used a distinctive bear spear (*gida*). In addition, they utilised bow and arrow and self-triggered arrows.

Much superstition prevailed among this heathen people. Every type of illness made them turn to a particular, appropriate fetish which they believed could offer protection. In front of their huts – which they called *fanse* – they mounted a bird on a high pole, a cuckoo carved from wood, named *gaza*, with its head facing the rising sun. And since no-one had ever found a cuckoo nest, they believed the *gaza* had come to Earth on a sunbeam to protect the habitats of men.

When I told them that the cuckoo was also to be found in Germany, and that it does not build nests but leaves its eggs in the nests of other birds, they thought I had lost my mind.

An idol of ebony, about one foot long, called Gangideumini, was kept in a secret place in the *fanse*. Gangideumini is the good spirit who protects the family against external, physical dangers. Kalgumaen, a two-foot long idol carved of poplar, is a daily reminder to the Goldes of their ancestors, who they believe were giants, and whom they honour, worship and find inspiration in.

It is precisely to honour their forefathers that the Golde people travel to a mountain by the lower course of the River Bikin (yet another of the many tributaries of the Ussuri), which has a certain manlike form and is supposed to represent a benign god, who grants both good health and luck in all forms of hunting. Some years later, at the foot of this mountain, I came across a host of offerings: small stones, coloured strips of cloth, and bowls with millet, tea, tobacco leaves and other items.

The Golde people also have other idols, amongst them the so-called *maulkain*, with its chest pierced with an arrow, placed in a tree near their cabins. The Goldes believe that sickness enters the body through a hole; therefore another hole is needed for it to exit, around the area about where the heart is situated.

Whilst hunting, Goldes carry two small fetishes in their belt, so-called *oetzichoe*, which they believe bring good luck on sable hunts. They always have a hunting knife (*kuzain*) on their belt as well as a crooked knife (*gerso*), the latter for the carving of all sorts of domestic utensils.

Their winter dress consists of a deerskin hat with the hide intact and a tuft of sable tail on top (*horokdo*), a coat (*araimi*) made of tanned fish skin, trousers (*daucsoiki*) and shoes (*funducktuota*), also made from fish skin – attire, as we could ourselves attest – that held up well even in the harshest cold.

In summer, one will often find the Golde people on rivers in small, lightweight boats (*saai*), which they construct of a frame covered with birchbark, always equipped with a fishing rod (*ussuminkani*) and fishing spear (*unkilko*), looking to catch carp, pike and other species.

But it is only when the vast amounts of salmon return upriver from the sea in August and September that the Goldes, with the help of large nets, catch the essential supplies for the winter for both themselves and their dogs (which they are very reliant on, both as a source of food and for hunting). The fish skin is tanned and coloured with pigments they find in the plant kingdom. We collected examples of most of the objects above and sent them to the Museum of Ethnology in Hamburg.

18

Like all East Asian peoples, the Goldes retain a shaman. In reality he has little more influence than a run-of-the-mill quack in Europe. It is more likely his own enrichment that drives the shaman's attempts to heal people with serious or incurable afflictions. He thinks he can bring the half dead back to full health with spells, accompanied by a frightful racket and a stifling and ever-present cloud of incense. The poor heathens have full faith in their shaman. And when one fails, another is usually brought in, often from far away, preferably one who is even more renowned. Most of the time he does not succeed either, and in such cases an even larger tribute is demanded.

The following observation may perhaps illustrate just how naïve many natives can be: a well-known miracle doctor was called to a sick child in a settlement we were staying at. There was a deathly quiet in the *fanse*. First, the shaman tried out a special incense that was supposed to keep the devil at bay, but which only made it hard for us to breathe and caused him to have a violent coughing fit. Then he donned a bearskin hat and proceeded to bang on a drum (*bubin*), doing his utmost to summon the good spirits with drum rolls and the jingling of a bell. Sweat poured down his face. When he was finished, he opened a pouch and took out a small fetish (a human figure) and tied it round the sick child's neck to protect him from death, as he explained in both Golde and Russian.

After the ceremony I went outside to get some fresh air. A Golde accompanied me out and told me – as though imparting a deep secret – that the great shaman was immune to all harm, even if shot he was able to spit out the bullet and continue on living as though nothing had happened.

The man himself had witnessed just such a miracle. I asked who had fired the shot and he answered:

"His helper."

So, a stupid trick, as far as I could gather; the shaman had placed a bullet in his mouth beforehand, and the helper had fired a blank.

The following summer, while searching for butterflies near another Golde settlement, I heard a terrible racket coming from one of the *fanse*. The noise only increased, so I went to investigate, and lying on the bed (*naren*) within, I found an emaciated woman with a lit pipe in her mouth, doubtless suffering from consumption and close to death. A shaman in a bearskin hat was standing at the foot of the bed, and beside him his helper was out of sight, hidden under a blanket. Again, the room was filled with that same overwhelming incense.

Assisted by drumming and bellringing, they wailed as loudly as they could. The valiant Goldes had placed their weapons – bear spears and arrows with newly sharpened heads – pointing up towards the sky to keep the devil at bay. Even though the shaman knew that the woman could not be saved, he collected two sable pelts, five pounds of millet and two pounds of tobacco before hopping onto his boat and returning to his village.

But then the despairing people turned to *me*. They had seen us running around the forest with butterfly net and sweep net, as well as hanging up our special linen sheets at night. Our cyanide jars no doubt added to our air of mystery. It proved quite a struggle to extricate myself from the situation in one piece, those good people wanted at any cost to make me into a miracle doctor. And the next morning the woman lay dead, the pipe still in her mouth.

19

We were warned by some Cossacks in the Khekhtsir Hills that a gang of escaped convicts had sought refuge in the area, not Honghuzi this time but Russians, and that a woman and child out gathering mushrooms had failed to return home, probably because they were either dead or abducted.

I had planned on pairing a Saturnia boisduvalii female – which I had hatched in captivity – with a wild male, and set out as soon as it was sundown to a clearing I had my eye on in the forest.

I was there waiting for the male to make an appearance when, well after midnight, my dog began to emit a low and persistent growl. I instructed him to be quiet, but then heard a soft, cracking sound and the Cossacks' warning came to mind. The steps drew closer, I saw the outline of a man and released the dog, who threw himself upon the figure, pulled him to the ground twice and inflicted several serious bites upon his thighs and lower legs, to the accompaniment of much yelling and screaming. But just at that moment, a boisduvalii landed beside my female. I managed to get both in my cage and lost all interest in the intruder, who seized the opportunity to disappear into the darkness.

*

In order to return home as quickly as possible with my catch, I took a shortcut through the grounds of a small chapel with a graveyard, my path taking me about thirty metres from a free-standing tower, where I caught sight of a suspicious light. I continued on to the village and told the eldest Cossack of my observation. He was a powerfully built and resolute man, and immediately asked me to show him the place.

I left the boisduvaliis in Henry's safekeeping and, equipped with a revolver each, the Cossack and I went back to the graveyard. The light in the tower was now extinguished and nothing stirred. But the Cossack kicked in the door at the base of the building and called out that whoever might be hiding up there should come down right away, unarmed, or we would shoot to kill.

Finally, after repeated threats, a man descended. His hands were immediately tied. We investigated the tower, but found no-one else and began to make our way back towards the village, where the Cossacks had, in the space of a few days, constructed a makeshift prison, consisting of a large crate with iron bars along one side, similar to the cage we had once built for the tiger Yascha.

Whilst passing the chapel, we noticed the door was ajar. Without hesitating, the Cossack entered and brought out two more men, who had some makeshift beds in there. Shortly thereafter we also managed to catch the man who had been savaged by my dog, his moaning had given him away. We found stolen altar items in his bag, and pious as the Cossack was he gave the wretch an extra punishment the following day. He was stripped naked and tied up in a boat, where he had to sit with his open wounds while mosquitoes swarmed around him until he passed out.

Three days later, a river steamer arrived to transport the prisoners back to the katorga camp they had escaped from. None of them, however, confessed to anything as regards the missing woman and child, and as far as I am aware the case was never solved. But Henry and I had great success with our boisduvalii pair, a total of thirty-three specimens made it through metamorphosis.

As we had no plans on wintering in the Khekhtsir region, and autumn was drawing close, we bartered for a boat in a Golde village and paddled up the Ussuri, before following its tributary, the Bikin, for two days for circa sixty versts.

There we followed the directions we had been given to a small wooden cabin on a hill next to an abandoned pioneer settlement. But it was not only that one winter, but three years in all we would stay in that vast region, roving about the hills, mountains and forests around the Ussuri, Bikin and Amur, almost like nomads. We moved from one abode to another, sleeping for long periods in a tent or under the open sky, governed only by the seasons and the course of nature.

20

One afternoon, while hunting birds, I heard some menacing sounds from a nearby grove. I hurried behind a tree but was unable to see anything untoward. Then, from a towering oak, high above the rest of the vegetation, leaves and twigs fell. I glanced up and discovered that two brown bears had built a sort of nest up there, in all likelihood to escape from the insects on the forest floor. I had previously noticed such huge twigged structures but had believed them to be eagle nests.

A few days later, an acquaintance of ours came paddling upriver, a Cossack named Gavrilov. We rarely saw people, so we offered him tea and bread and sat talking for a while. Both Henry and I spoke good Russian by this time, although Henry was the more proficient – I had, after all, been living in near isolation on Askold for a long period while he had been in Vladivostok.

I happened to mention the "bear nest", and Gavrilov, responding in animated fashion, related a story about a friend who on his way home from haymaking last summer had been crossing the Ussuri by boat when halfway over he saw a bear swimming through the water. Gavrilov's friend was not armed, but paddled towards the bear all the same, in the hope that it would cling on to the boat, so he might ferry it to the far bank where his comrades, who were armed, could be found.

But Bruin the bear was not content just to hold on to the vessel. After much ado and great exertion, he was up *in* the boat, shaking the water off his fur. He did not display, however, any sign of intending to attack. About one hundred metres from the bank, where a number of onlookers had begun to form, amongst them the Cossack's comrades with their rifles, the bear decided enough was enough and launched himself back into the water, almost taking the Cossack along with him as the vessel listed, and swam back to the far bank, to the sound of rifles being fired in the air and applause from those gathered on the shore.

Gavrilov was planning on paddling upriver to an area he thought would prove to be good hunting ground for deer. He was armed with an old muzzleloader, which was suitable for harmless game. But for one reason or another he did not want to bring his dog, so that stayed behind with us and sat the rest of the day on the riverbank howling, as if filled with a sense of foreboding. In the meantime we continued on with our work, the preparation of a few species of duck and an old male wolverine (*Gulo gulo*, which incidentally means "glutton"), that Henry had bagged with a self-triggered bolt less than a verst from the cabin.

The previous winter we had adopted three jays (*Garrulus brandtii*) who, attracted by all our lard and offal, had become so tame that one day they simply flew into the house and perched on the edge of my bed so all I had to do was close the door.

At first, we kept them in the same cage, but they fought so much that feathers flew, so after a time one of them had to forfeit his life. The remaining two were placed in a cage each but even then made such a commotion that we had to let one go. It refused to take permanent leave of the cabin however, and continued to fly in and out, as though to torment and tease his companion who was still incarcerated.

We also had a hawfinch (*Coccothraustes japonicus*) which I had winged and later nursed back to health. The wounds healed quickly but it refused to leave us and had become quite domesticated, alighting on our shoulders and hands as we cured skins, waiting for scraps of meat, and also joining us at mealtimes to be given fruit pips. We had named him Jakob, and he had no need of a cage. During the day he would fly out the open door, flutter around the deciduous woodland, and return when it suited him. But he never allowed us to take him in our hands, we received feisty pecks from his powerful bill if we tried.

We decided it was high time to release the last jay. It took off, in its characteristic undulating way, landing on a white birch by the house, and began to chatter. Then it flitted over the river before disappearing in the vegetation on the far side. It turned up a few hours later, however, and tapped on the window with its beak, so we let it in again to help itself to the wolverine fat Henry had provided. Afterwards it took to its cage for a well-deserved sleep – I only mention all these trivial matters to describe our normal working day. But the end of this day proved anything but trivial. As darkness fell, Gavrilov's boat came into sight drifting downriver. It was only when it reached the bank that we saw our friend on board, lying flat on his back in the bilge. He was known as the strongest and most seasoned Cossack in Ussuri, but was now bloodier and more mauled than I had seen any living man, and had obviously encountered a bear. Fortunately he had been able to paddle downstream, otherwise we would never have seen him again.

We managed to get him inside. The dog was completely hysterical. I found the bandages and dressings, cleaned his wounds and cauterised them with creolin water (creosote). His neck, arms, chest and back had taken the worst of it, and several of the wounds required fifteen or twenty stitches. But even though the bear had embedded his fangs in his skull, the poor man had remained conscious the entire time. We gave him several good mouthfuls of spirits, but only after suffering through an agonising night, was he able to relate the dramatic account of what had occurred.

He told us he had gone in the direction of the "bear nest" I had informed him about, but only because he was tracking an elk, he avowed, when a dark figure had risen up in the man-high grass. He had fired in the belief it was the elk, a reflex action. But the next moment, only a metre from him, a bear had appeared on its hind legs – no doubt as flabbergasted as Gavrilov – and hurled himself through the gun smoke of a second shot.

This too failed to hit its target, and having no opportunity to reload, the Cossack had tried to draw his knife, but this was hanging on a cord behind his back, so he had to resort to using his hands and arms. Although the bear was taller than him, he managed to get it by the throat and squeeze for several minutes. The bear had groaned and whined, but eventually managed to come free and sink its fangs into his head. At that point all Gavrilov's strength completely deserted him. He fell to the ground and attempted to protect his head with his mutilated arms, and it was in this position that he incurred the brutal bites to the back of the neck. But bears find human flesh foul, so it had ended the set-to by giving his victim's legs a quick sniff before ambling off. When all was quiet, Gavrilov had managed, just about, to crawl back down to the boat.

He mumbled, with wounded pride, that if only the bear had not had those damned teeth and claws, he would surely have managed to strangle it with just his bare hands.

And he kept repeating this over the course of the week he spent with us, until a contingent of Cossacks came paddling upriver to search for him.

They took him back to civilisation, where reportedly he soon recovered. But, by all accounts, he never grew tired of asserting that if only that damned bear had not had such sharp teeth and claws, then . . . He did not understand how this type of talk served to ruin his heroic reputation. People began to poke fun at him. And Gavrilov began drinking more and more frequently, and one day during the summer after the drama at Bikin he declared – while three sheets to the wind – that the time was right, yes indeed, for him to go on a bear hunt again. His friends had merely laughed. But Gavrilov left, never to return from that hunt, and neither was he ever found. In time, his comrades erected a cross in the graveyard by the camp, with the inscription: "The hero Gavrilov does not lie at rest beneath this cross. Nobody knows when he was born, or when he died."

Both of the jays we had freed stayed in the area as long as we were there, even perching at night in their old cages, which were always open. Jakob the hawfinch, on the other hand, disappeared shortly after Gavrilov's week on his sickbed, and it was a curious departure: he sat awhile in the sunlight on the floor in the middle of the room, as though to enjoy the warmth or ponder something or other. Then he walked slowly but determinedly over the threshold, out onto the steps and sat there, as if to weigh things up once again. He looked one last time over his shoulder and took off, never to return, probably having picked up the scent of a partner or a congener.

21

In October we could come across bears in mountainous mixed forest, usually traversing the vegetation on the hunt for honey. I followed after one who stopped along its way to raise himself up on tree after tree, before eventually being rewarded for all the effort and zeroing in on an oak tree about a metre thick. He began clawing furiously around the hole, which was not more than thirty centimetres above the ground, and was immediately attacked by thousands of angry bees. They penetrated his fur, and his eyes and snout were not spared either. The bear held his paws over its face to protect himself against the furious insects.

When the number of bees was sufficiently reduced, he investigated the tree, tearing open a hole with his teeth and claws large enough for him to get his paws in. Honeycomb, honey and bees were scooped out and devoured. A meal like this weighs as much as eighty pounds, without causing the bear's stomach any trouble. For a human on the other hand, the honey of wild bees is only edible in small and diluted amounts, owing to the presence of many toxins.

The bees' hole is usually located two or three metres above the ground, and generally in an old woodpecker hole. This makes it very difficult for the bear to empty the trunk. I witnessed first-hand how two Russian hunters exploited the bear's predicament to obtain both bear and honey, using a particular method, which was widespread, they informed me:

First, they sealed the opening so as not to be bothered by the bees, then hammered nails in a circle around the hole, cut the heads off them with pliers, before sharpening them with a file. A little way out on a solid branch a couple of metres above the hole they tied a rope, which they used to raise a platform made from wooden planks until it was about a metre lower than the hole, attaching it to the trunk with a thin cord.

Let us now say that a bear that has been trying in vain to get hold of honey for several days, wanders past and discovers the platform. It soon clambers up and sets to work on the beehive, but cuts itself on the nails and becomes angry. The cord holding the platform gives, the seat and bear swing out from the tree, and oddly enough the bear does not think of jumping down, but stays there gaping, just waiting for the hunter.

People in the region around Amur did not hunt the Asian black bear at this time. But once in a while a young bear was taken by a tiger. Normally tigers only attacked elderly bears, and preferably when they were wounded or suffering from illness.

In my opinion, the bear is the most interesting and most good-natured inhabitant of the Siberian wilderness. It usually roams around peacefully, on the hunt for berries, leaves and insects. But it has an unstable disposition and when frightened can, in a matter of seconds, lose its temper.

One morning after snow had fallen, I was hunting deer when I came upon the tracks of a very large bear who must have been taken by surprise by the snow and likely not had time to organise its den. I followed the tracks until it grew dark, and then with a heavy heart, had to give up.

I forgot about the entire affair, but in the spring we were wandering through the same area when our dog came across the remains of a colossal bear (*Ursus behringiana*), and ten paces away from it the carcass of a powerful tiger, both dead from the wounds they had inflicted upon each other. All the meat had been devoured over the course of the winter by other tigers, wolves, foxes and birds. The skull of the bear was forty-eight centimetres long and almost as wide. After arranging the bones we measured the length of the animal at 2.89 metres. We also laid out the tiger bones and they stretched over four metres. The tiger's pelt was very badly damaged, but we were able to cure and sew it together to some extent, and the sad remains – along with the bones – went to a museum in England.

One day, having had equipped myself with a black umbrella and a stick to beat larvae from the bushes, I heard a pronounced footfall. A bear emerged from a narrow gully and was headed straight at me. In all likelihood we were both equally surprised, and in order to deter it from coming any closer, I opened and closed the umbrella quickly and repeatedly. This threw the forest dweller completely off balance. It leaped backwards, and lay on the ground flailing for a few moments before getting back up and hurrying off in the opposite direction. Henry almost split his sides laughing when I related the episode.

In the three-thousand-foot-high mountains around Bikin I discovered a species of deer with slightly shorter legs as well as less body mass in general than the Siberian roe deer (*Capreolus pygargus*), which moves in the deciduous forests and has a grey coat in the winter.

This new deer has a rusty-red coat in both summer and winter and is never found in deciduous woodlands. I managed to shoot four specimens of the species, and prepare and send the hides to Europe. Unfortunately, I have never found out which museums they ended up in. I suspect they are described as *Capreolus pygargus* in summer coat, but that would be incorrect, so in the event that this more diminutive species are yet to be described, I give it the name *Capreolus doerriesi*, in honour of my brother.

22

The autumn storms once again swept the foliage from the trees and the migratory birds headed for warmer climes. They resemble a Swiss timepiece in relation to their precision and sense for the changing seasons. The snowstorms then arrived, burying our little cabin completely in a matter of days.

After removing some planks from the roof, we were able to creep out and shovel snow into a two-metre high embankment around the house, sheltering it from the wind.

Now that the landscape was encrusted in snow and ice and the Bikin was frozen, it was possible to travel faster. With six dogs and a sleigh we made it after a long day's journey upriver on the ice to one of the Oroch villages. The Oroch people are another interesting tribe, who to a certain extent resemble the Goldes.

They also build their houses from mud and heat them by means of a channel leading from a fire outside; the heat is drawn through the dwelling and expelled out the roof via a hollow tree trunk. The winter dress of the Orochs consists of a hat (*bogdo*) and a jacket (*lugdemon-taga*) sewn from tanned deerskin. They generally wear a vest of elk skin (*schiga*) over this. Their trousers (*ouiti*), also of deerskin, are tied around the ankles. Shoes (*nilimounta*) are sewn of leather. But also here we saw garments of tanned fish skin. The women dressed in a similar fashion and loved jewellery; their ears, arms, wrists and braided hair were always adorned with pearls and silver chains.

The first time we encountered the Orochs we had the impression we were dealing with Indians. They worshipped various gods, just like the Goldes, and one finds innumerable – also animal-like – idols and fetishes in their huts as well as in the forest around their villages. The Orochs have great stamina and are brave hunters. Not even the women, who often accompany the men on hunts, will shy away from taking on a bear.

Not long after we had settled into one particular Oroch village, we were sought out by a man who had been mauled by a bear. His hat, vest and jacket were soaked in blood.

We cleaned his wounds with the equipment we always brought along, and gave him new clothes – we ourselves always dressed like the natives. He told us how he, along with two companions, had stumbled upon the winter den of a she-bear, and a pregnant she-bear sleeps lightly just prior to the cubs being born in January. As he unwittingly drew closer, she had suddenly thrown herself upon him, and, as he said:

"It happened so fast I didn't have time to use my spear, but fortunately my companions used theirs, and after a long fight, they got the better of her."

During our stay with the Orochs, we collected a considerable amount of ethnographic objects, which we later sold to various museums in Europe. Their cradles were particularly interesting. They were passed from generation to generation and were filled with fetishes, donated by relatives to protect the child. Golde and Oroch infants spend the first years of their lives exposed to a constant jangling and tinkling in their ears, which is meant to prepare them for the silence of the forests.

As mentioned previously, at this time, modern firearms were not used by the Golde, nor by the Orochs or Gilyaks, who all live in the region around Amur. All three groups killed their prey in a traditional manner, with bow and arrow in an open hunt and always on foot, by quite simply sneaking up on the animals. In addition they used both a large and a smaller variety of crossbow. Where elk and deer had their crossing places, self-triggering constructions were rigged, not in this case with firearms either, but with a particularly large crossbow.

We utilised this method ourselves – with an extra strong steel bow – and brought down both pine marten (*Martes martes*) and a stoat. We also took many wolves and foxes in the same way. Across small, frozen mountain streams we hung scraps of meat Oroch-style in trees, some twenty or thirty centimetres apart. The crossbow was mounted on the opposite bank at two or three paces from the bait. From the bait to the trigger ran a thin thread that released the bolt.

Many of the peoples in the Amur and Ussuri regions also dug pitfalls. First a number of trees were felled and trunks and branches arranged so they formed a gate of sorts through the forest, with certain narrow openings, where a pit as narrow as possible was dug, which was covered with twigs, leaves and grass. When a deer or a wild boar fell down into the hole, it found itself in such a tight squeeze that it could not manage to get up again. A bear, however, could scrape and dig at the walls with such desperation and for so long that the pit would fill with enough earth for it to regain its freedom.

I fell into such a pitfall myself once. Fortunately it was old and partially filled with leaves and soil. All the same, I struggled for over five hours before getting back out.

23

In addition to the deer Cervus lühdorfi, that is Isubra, which is found along the lengths of the Amur and Ussuri, I brought down a lone, odd, wapiti-like deer by Bikin. Judging by the colours, it was undescribed. The body was silver-grey; the legs, head, and neck were dark brown and the speculum white as chalk. Only on one occasion since have I seen a similar animal, in England of all places, at the private zoological gardens of the Duke of Bedford, at Woburn Abbey, though I was unable to learn from where the specimen came, Lord Bedford did not know himself. Judging by the antlers I would presume it more Cervus wollichi affinis than the Asian wapiti.

I caught the rare specimen as it was growing dark, and as I had no horse could not bring the carcass with me. There were both old and fresh tiger tracks all about me in the terrain, so I buried the deer in the snow in the hope of returning with a horse and sleigh the following day to collect it.

But it snowed so heavily that night that moving outdoors the next morning was impossible. It was three whole days before I was able to return, and about sixty paces from the deer my horse must have got the scent of a tiger because it grew uneasy, began to snort, stamp its hooves, and would not move a step further. I tethered it to a tree and sneaked closer, and the old nag was not wrong: a tiger had dug the deer out, dragged it about fifty metres away and was lying down enjoying the carrion.

There was no room for hesitation, I took aim and was ready to fire. But the animal turned to look at me in the same instant and his head covered his carotid artery, so we remained lying, staring at one another, waiting. Then he suddenly rose up, as if preparing to pounce, giving me a clear shot at the neck again and I squeezed the trigger.

The tiger leaped in my direction, thrashed around in the snow, and lost the lustre in his eyes shortly after.

I had to throw a blanket over the beast in order to bring the horse over to the scene. Of the rare deer, only the antlers and head remained. And I have not managed to identify the species since. But the tiger came home to the cabin to be skinned and prepared, and I also took care of the skull.

Usually new skeletons are constructed from plasticine or plaster in the museums where the animals are stuffed. But there was also a certain demand for craniums for scientific studies. Preparing them was however no simple task, because after the hide is removed and the largest lumps of flesh scraped off, the skull must be boiled to loosen the last remnants. And it was seldom we were in possession of pots big enough for tigers and the larger bears. But we were able to borrow a steel trough from the Orochs that could be placed over a fire.

It turned out a very clean and lovely object. It did not however end up in the hands of any scientist, but at an inn in Vladivostok, at our old friend Hans Gammenthaler's to be precise, who as soon as he set

eyes upon it, wanted to purchase it to hang on the wall of his estab-
lishment. A dazzling white tiger skull mounted on a mahogany board,
with mouth open and all its teeth intact, right next to a cuckoo clock:
Gammenthaler never made any attempt to disguise his Swiss origins.
Now he had the most spectacular ornament in the city to boast of. He
paid me six hundred roubles for the skull, a sum I would return to him
over time in board and lodging.

24

One day in January we registered a temperature of forty-nine degrees below zero, and I have never experienced a cold like it anywhere else. Even in the forests, where the wind could not take hold, I found winter birds like the goldcrest (*Regulus regulus*) and the wood nuthatch (*Sitta europaea*) frozen solid in the snow. In such conditions, a hunter will feel his blood stiffen in his veins if he is not in constant movement and does not take all other manner of precaution – avoid touching metal, blink continuously, and clothe and behave as the natives do. We actually learned a great deal from the natives, and have much to be grateful to them for. They were also our best source of information with regard to flora, fauna, geology and meteorology.

Fortunately, during the worst of the cold period we had enough to do preparing in the *fanse* we had borrowed. We worked on beasts of prey, rodents and birds, and curiously enough these months turned out to be extremely productive.

But even the harshest winter must end sometime. It grew brighter and milder, the ice thawed and water ran on the sunnier slopes – the change always came as a surprise to us; some days could begin with intense cold and then fade with sweeping föhn winds. And at the beginning of

March we packed the yield of the winter hunts on the sleighs, bade the Orochs farewell and set off downriver again toward the cabin, and just in the nick of time I might add, because the ice on the Bikin broke up early that year.

Such a break-up of ice is, incidentally, a natural wonder. Happily back in the log cabin we now had front row seats, viewing it just ten or twelve paces from the riverbank, which fortunately was high enough up in the terrain, because in a matter of mere minutes what for months had been solid ground beneath our feet completely disintegrated. Slabs of ice broke against one another with a violent crash, the floes piling up and collapsing together again, larger and smaller masses of ice tearing into parts of the bank, taking soil, bushes and trees along with them. It all lasted over twenty-four hours. On affected stretches the landscape was radically transformed, with new river courses created, and yet another unique spring could begin.

As usual, we dedicated the next few months to insects. Amongst other things, I made some interesting observations of the Camberwell Beauty (*Vanessa antiopa*). This beautiful butterfly usually appears in flocks of up to forty or fifty specimens (in captivity somewhat fewer) in order to protect eggs, pupae and larvae from mosquitos and other hostile insects who attempt to lay their own eggs on the vulnerable pupae. Interlopers are chased away by the Vanessas, who form a military unit that not only protects their own progeny, but also those of congeners, the cooperation is impressive to witness.

Even more impressive were the larval defences: thirty to forty specimens can sit together on a leaf and beat the forefront of their forms in lockstep on its surface, causing it to flutter as though from the wind, making it impossible for parasites to land.

We bred several Vanessas, and when they eventually crept from the pupae and we offered them freedom, they refused to quit the catch box. The few who eventually did depart returned repeatedly, to sit awhile on the empty pupal shell, and could take two or three such farewells before finally breaking away from their childhood homes; behaviour we also recorded amongst other species on Askold.

In the course of this season we were able to add many rare or hitherto unknown species to the collection. A hawk moth in the Erebidae family amongst others, which was later named after us – Catocala doerriesi – Staudinger again bestowing this honour on us, and it lives only here in East Siberia, as far as I am aware, a fine thought for us personally. Our yield of birds was also particularly large this summer. And early in the autumn we packed the boat to the gills and made ready to depart Bikin.

On the first leg we allowed ourselves to be led leisurely downstream to the Bikin's confluence with the Ussuri, in a state of sheer laziness – pipe smoking, reading and drawing. But the following morning odd cries reached us from a wooded area along the bank, the sound of groaning and lamentations.

We paddled over and found a young Golde, not more than eighteen years old, so terribly ravished by ticks and insects that he barely resembled a human. He was sitting on the ground against a tree, his hands and feet bound, and only with great effort managed to tell us that the village shaman had condemned him to starve to death. When we asked what he had done, he answered:

"I'm in the habit of lying and stealing."

Our hearts went out to the poor wretch and we untied him, boiled some tea, gave him bread and kept him company for a while. I advised him not to return to his village but rather to seek out another. His response was equivocal, so I doubt he saw this as an option. We gave him provisions for four days, said goodbye and continued down to the Ussuri. When we arrived we sold the boat, carried our baggage aboard a river steamer and sailed upriver for three days to a small village where we obtained a horse and wagon and made our way to our old headquarters in Baranovsky, by the River Suifun, planning to winter there.

25

We were in the area the Russians call Tigrovo Paid. For once, on the first day of the new year, we ventured out together, and soon spotted a twenty-metre-high dead oak, with an gap right at the base. On the snow outside lay piles of fresh earth and bark, indicating the possible presence of something alive within. Judging by the enormous girth of the tree, it could only be a bear.

I loaded the rifle, bent over and looked down into the tree – right at the fur of a she-bear who spun around at the very same moment, apparently ready to attack. As our fat reserves were low, I fired a shot and drew back quickly.

A terrible commotion ensued within. It seemed as though the whole tree was going to split open, before the she-bear exploded out in a fury and began staggering about in the snow. Henry then fired a shot and she tumbled down a slope, coming to a stop at the foot of a tree and lying quite still.

It was impossible to transport the four hundred and fifty pound carcass back to the post, but the presence of wolves and tigers meant we could not leave it where it was, so even though it was now dark, we began dragging and rolling the animal downhill towards the nearest ravine.

When the terrain levelled out somewhat, I went to fetch the horse and sleigh whilst Henry stayed with the bear. Two hours later I returned in bright moonlight. The snow-covered ridges lay still around us. The moon smiled down through the tops of the old pines while we laboured to get the huge animal up onto the sleigh and tie it down. And it was quite the moonlight ride. The horse stumbled, losing its balance constantly in the deep snow, and was exhausted by the time we reached the next valley floor, where fortunately the going got a bit easier, and we were back at the log cabin well before dawn.

We placed the bear in a secure stall, slept for a few hours, then got down to the flaying. First, we removed the entrails and dragged them to the nearest ditch, as we were wont to do, setting the table for hungry woodland birds, crows, tits, ravens and eagles – we had also observed some interesting great grey shrikes eating there.

After the skin was removed, we melted the fat in an iron pot standing on three stones over a fire. The parts which did not melt down we poured out in the snow – yet more birdfeed. And we had just put aside what parts were fit for human consumption when five Koreans turned up, all with baskets on their backs, filled with tobacco, on their way to the closest town. They had walked through deep snow all the way from Korea, I do not know for how many days, and in broken Russian announced that they were ravenous and asked if they could have the offal, which of course we could not refuse them.

They unfastened their baskets, sat down with gusto and had in the space of a half-hour filled their stomachs with the discarded leftovers, without bread or salt, whereupon they stood up rather heavily, heaved their carrying baskets on their backs again, thanked us and continued on their way.

Henry and I looked at each other in amazement, wondering how on earth they could digest such stodgy fare. They left with at least three pounds each in their stomachs. The she-bear weighed four hundred and fifty pounds, as I mentioned, and approximately one hundred and sixty of this was pure lard.

She also had two near full-term cubs in her womb, leading me to conclude that Asian black bears breed in and around the middle of January. This was also evident from her teats, which were already swollen and full of milk.

26

As noted, she-bears do not sleep very deeply just prior to giving birth, and they will clean their den a number of times. The male, however, slumbers so heavily that one can get close enough to plunge a spear into him. As far as I have been able to observe, the male is as plump on leaving his den in the spring as he was when going in to hibernate at the start of autumn. But he loses this fat in the space of a short time in an intense search for food, of which there is not much to be found in the first days of spring. And when we collected butterflies in prairie-like areas like this, with one-and-a-half-metre-high grass and perennials, the bear was actually a welcome guest, ploughing through the vegetation sending all sorts of insects fluttering up, making them easy prey for us as we followed behind with nets.

Owing to the shortage of food, all species of bear here are obliged to remain in hibernation from the beginning of November to a little way into March. First the brown bear and the giant Bruin make a sort of pointed tent located, for example, in the cavity of a pine uprooted by the wind. Then they gather various materials and seal the den from the inside. The snow will fall and blanket the entire dwelling, making it snug and warm.

*

In an interlude from insect collecting, I had to go hunting one day for food, and found myself on quite high ground running below a rockface, when I entered a narrow ravine which ended in a scree. There I came upon two bear cubs, no bigger than cats, at play. The mother must have heard me, because I heard a sharp call of alarm before the cubs disappeared immediately into the mass of loose stones.

But why did the she-bear not show herself?

I fired a shot into the air and a wild snorting head emerged into the daylight. But only the head, because the half-starved animal was, despite her efforts, unable to exit through the narrow opening, due to an arrangement of sharp stones blocking her path. She had most likely entered this trap the previous autumn. We did not usually hunt bear in the spring, but I was concerned for the cubs and shot the she-bear to save them from also starving to death.

But there was no way of retrieving her from the scree, so I had to clamber in and gut her inside the den, and even then I only just managed to manoeuvre the carcass out.

I fetched the horse and dragged the animal home. The following day I returned and, after much effort, managed to get hold of the bear cubs. They had remained in the area and no doubt believed the chase they led me round and round on was some sort of game. I led them each home on a leash, sold one to a passing Russian who wanted to teach it circus skills, and kept the other.

I named it Mischka and we became very good friends. He slept in the cabin with us for over a year, in a wooden stall I built for him, or more of a bed really, stuffed with the same straw we ourselves slept on. He joined me each day when I went out to collect butterflies. I also trained him up to accompany me while hunting, at the same time as I was training up a new dog, Fingauka, as the last one had succumbed to the cold the previous winter. And the training was a success, I must say.

Not only did Mischka rouse all manner of interesting insects from the vegetation, but he also fetched downed ducks in shallow water just as effectively, and with as much determination, as Fingauka, with whom, incidentally, he developed a very close relationship. When Mischka was in a good mood he also found deer. The only thing that unsettled him, even when fully matured, was tigers. He would almost break down when we came across fresh tiger tracks, press up close to me, stand up on his hind legs and stretch out his paws with pleading eyes for me to take him over my shoulders like I used to when he was a cub. The last time I experienced this he weighed well over a hundred kilos. I am sure we were quite a sight.

One day, I was busy in the mixed forest collecting beetles, and as usual Mischka was helping, albeit more to his own advantage now; no sooner did he get hold of a thick leaf beetle than he would stuff it in his mouth instead of leaving it for his master.

An ominous cracking sound from not too far off suddenly reached my ears, and Mischka and Fingauka also paused and stood stock still. But while the dog sought shelter between my legs, Mischka raised his snout to sniff the air in all directions – so I could exclude a tiger in any case. Then he seemed to reach a decision, raced off and disappeared. I called out to him, used all the words we had trained on and he responded to, even the whistles, and Fingauka yapped and barked like he did when they were play fighting.

But that was the last we saw of Mischka. He had likely caught the scent of another bear, and I suppose he preferred the company of his own kind to playing house with humans and dogs. There was nothing for it but to let our friend go, but we did so with heavy hearts.

Fortunately I had Fingauka, the most capable hound I ever had, to mourn the loss with. I had purchased him in a Golde village, and the Goldes usually let their bitches free to roam in the forest when they are on heat, in the hope they'll mate with wolves. Fingauka was in fact half-wolf. He obeyed my slightest command, never flushed a bird too quickly, retrieved nearly everything I shot down, and responded to mere nods and hand signals when we had to move soundlessly through terrain. He was also the only dog I consistently spoke Russian to. One particular incident made me wonder if he had special powers:

We had been roaming around looking for larvae and beetles since early morning, and as nightfall was approaching, we decided to take a route home round a hill where the terrain appeared more promising. But the detour turned out to take a lot longer than we had envisaged, we were without food or firearms, and the pangs of hunger were becoming harder to stave off. Then we spotted a pheasant atop a bushy tree, about four metres high. Fingauka promptly sat down and began baying most mournfully, a wolf howl in the middle of summer, and the pheasant froze but did not take off, staring intently down at the dog instead, as though in a trance.

Whispering to each other, we hatched a plan. I crept under the bush and began to whittle away at the trunk. The tree was perhaps five or six centimetres thick down at the root where I was working, so it took time, and Fingauka sat the entire time holding the bird mesmerised with his strange song. Eventually I cut right through the trunk and lowered the tree slowly and methodically down, still without any reaction on the bird's part, until it was only a metre above the forest floor, at which point Henry was close enough to strike it with the hazel walking stick he had held at the ready. Not long afterwards we were sitting around a fire sharing an exquisite pheasant dish for three. It is one of the most curious hunting stories I can remember.

After this episode Henry was also keen to acquire a Golde dog. He got two, a male and a female. The bitch died though, from a snakebite, shortly after she arrived at the house, but the male developed quickly and got on well with Fingauka. We viewed them after a time as brothers, which they probably did as well.

Over the course of that winter they learned to work very well together, dividing up the terrain effectively between themselves and displaying a lupine sense for coordinated hunting. They could also communicate with one another over long distances. Henry named his dog Leon, and Leon suffered from a similar debility to Mischka the bear – he was terrified of tigers. It was impossible to make him cross a tiger's tracks, no matter how much time and energy Henry spent trying to get him accustomed to it, this was after all a land abundant in tigers. At night, Leon and Fingauka slept in Mischka's old bed.

At the beginning of April the following year we believed that spring had arrived; here and there the bushes were already brightening up, assuming a weak green tinge; life was making a shy return, and birdsong once again filled mind and soul. But then a sudden snowstorm laid the land under a new winter. A couple of days later, I was on my way home after inspecting a pine marten trap when I came across tiger tracks not more than forty paces from the cabin. Henry was off elsewhere with both dogs, so I fetched a gun and went back out alone to track the beast, which was no problem in the snow. But once again I had to give up when darkness descended. And the next day it proved too late: the snow melted so quickly in the spring sunshine that not even Fingauka was able to follow the tracks. Although I ought to mention he was not overly fond of tigers either, so it is possible he hoodwinked his master in this instance.

Sable were not to be found in Tigrovo. But the Cervus lühdorfi and the somewhat smaller Dybowski species of red deer dwelled in the region. The Dybowski would play a crucial role for me later in life. We encountered it everywhere and became very au fait with how it roamed the landscape. We also captured stoats, mostly along small mountain streams in forests on higher ground.

If one follows the tracks of a stoat in winter, one can expect to be led to a tree with a hive of wild bees. The elegant predator will scratch around the entrance, and the bees will do their best to chase him off, resulting in their freezing to death in the cold, whereupon the stoat will consume them and take up residence in the available cavity. I have repeatedly found the remains of bees among the contents of the stomachs of stoats.

The large yellow-throated marten (*Martes flavigula*) was seldom to be seen. Badger (*Meles leucurus amurensis*) and raccoon dog (*Nyctereutes viverrinus*) on the other hand were everywhere to be found. We also encountered ground squirrels; when frightened, the colourful rodents stood up on their hind legs and looked almost like little humans.

We trapped a total of five specimens of the large wildcat civet (*Viverricula pallida*), which can grow to over a metre long. Wild boar in herds were not an uncommon sight, and then a tiger would not be far behind. Very occasionally we came across the tracks of the Amur leopard (*Panthera pardus orientalis*), which likes to lie motionless in trees or on cliffs waiting for prey to pass, preferably a species of red deer.

27

We had plans of paying the island of Askold another visit this summer, as it was yet to be fully explored. So once again we packed up our painstakingly collected objects in trunks which we sealed and loaded on the wagon. We then drove to Vladivostok to lodge with our old friend Hans Gammenthaler. He said what he always said when we arrived, how he had not dreamed he would see us alive again, that we looked like savages, smelled like savages and were both considerably older. He himself was a little rounder, his complexion even whiter, I do not think he spent much time outdoors. He had also lost what little he had had of hair since our last meeting.

In the past few years, an increasing number of Russians had come to the city, with all manner of adventurous purpose, be it trade, hunting, exploration or more shady activities. More foreigners also: Europeans, Chinese, Japanese, Americans. New buildings had sprouted up, and in the port sailboats and steamers lay side by side, as well as whaling ships and a considerable fishing fleet. Vladivostok is a strange and diverse city, built without order and design. I have previously used the word "streets", but none of them provided any guidance with name or numbers, rather they were alleyways or paths that had arisen between randomly located buildings.

A letter, sent from Europe a year and a half ago, was waiting for me at Gammenthaler's. It was from none other than Otto Staudinger, the entomologist who was the recipient of the bulk of our insect collections. And to my great delight he was full of praise for the specimens we had gathered; he was particularly happy with the butterflies, which were of the highest quality, he asserted, amongst the best he had ever received, and he had collectors working for him all across the globe.

This missive was certainly stimulating but also somewhat peculiar, considering he paid for these consignments and would hardly encourage us to raise our prices. But it did not dent our desire for fresh quests.

We sent off what we had brought with us from Suifun, Bikin and Amur, and immediately got down to equipping ourselves for the expedition to Askold. But we could not bring the dogs, nor could we give them away, like we usually did, so we left them in a kennel Gammenthaler erected on the spot between his pigsty and stable. He had a way with animals. Then we went aboard a Chinese junk that was to take us to the island. The captain demanded a high price and it was no easy voyage.

The lack of an engine and adverse wind conditions resulted in the crossing taking two whole days.

When we made land it was hard work getting the equipment ashore at the landing place on the north of the island, due to rough seas and even more wind. A junk is not an elegant or easily manoeuvrable craft by any means. But we soon found the dwelling Wanka and I had built, spent a few days fixing it up, and were in full swing with our work by April 27.

The forest had acquired a light grey-green hue and was brightened up here and there by cherry blossoms (*Prunus sp.*), their pink petals the butterfly collector's most cherished sign of spring. We had plans to once again breed a selection of butterflies from the larval stage, work we were really beginning to get the hang of.

Askold is exceptionally fertile. One morning I dug up a spadeful of soil in search of beetles and larvae and had just begun examining one beetle when I discovered there was no more soil left, or rather to be more precise, it was not earth I had dug up, but insects, who had awakened and now ran away.

A species of Parnassius exists with the taxon Parnassius bremeri, which is native to the steep, rocky slopes here, and usually drawn to the sedum plant. Even though it had been described twenty years previously (by Bremer), it was very rare and featured in few collections. That summer we only got hold of a few specimens, but would later catch many more on the mainland; as a matter of fact, they were some of our most important finds.

One day I came upon a particularly beautiful, bright variant. I swung the net at it, tripped and tumbled down between some stones, but did not take my eyes off the butterfly and watched closely as it corkscrewed up along a six-metre-high rockface before alighting on a swaying blade of grass. With the net in my belt, I followed after by way of a rocky gully. The higher I went the more demanding it became, and when I finally thought I could swing my net, the stone I was standing on gave way. I slid several metres down. My face and hands took the brunt of it, but miraculously I managed to grab on to some oak twigs and save myself at the last moment. And as luck would have it, the butterfly was still in the net.

The butterflies fluttering from flower to flower in the sunlight revealed the true face of the island. Along the sheer sea cliffs, I observed the large, lustrous green swallowtail Papilio maackii. Like an eagle, it can twist skyward then veer off and continue hundreds of metres out over the sea, before turning and going back to the rocky shore, where it is apt to land on a leaf of the Amur cork tree (*Phellodendron amurense*), the larvae's primary host plant.

While searching for precisely these larvae, I was witness to a spectacle of quite a different order: a whale swam in close to the beach below where I was working. By rolling from side to side it "crawled" right up onto the foreshore. Powerful fins raised up stones the size of a man's head in seething foam with thunderous noise.

It managed to manoeuvre itself one hundred and eighty degrees around and lay with its head facing out. I moved behind some rocks to admire it through my field glasses, a giant of some fifteen metres in length, with a third of its form above the surface. A grey whale (*Eschrichtius robustus*), as far as I could make out, weighing more than fifteen tonnes. The species renowned to have the most beautiful song.

On closer inspection I noticed a large number of parasites which it was trying to scrape off on the rocky bottom. After ten or fifteen minutes of intensive effort it began to move off, manoeuvring itself back out to sea the same way it came, and vanished into the deep with a final colossal beat of its tailfin.

Several days later I made a rare observation of the mating ritual of the same species of whale from atop a five-hundred-foot-high cliff. It developed into quite a vigorous frolic – the male ramming the female from below so that both of them actually stood dancing in the air over the surface of the water, only to fall back in a splashing, foaming mass.

As their bodies emerged from below for a third time, the linkage seemed to have come about.

In the hope of experiencing that fantastic sight again, I returned to my viewing point that same afternoon. It proved a long wait but eventually I caught sight of the two leviathans. Only now they lay calmly side by side on the undulating surface, looking like two islands adrift.

28

When we were children, our father would tell us about the metamorphoses of the butterfly: a human resembles a human from the embryonic stage right up into old age, as most species resemble themselves. The larva of the butterfly, on the other hand, bears very few similarities to a pupa, and a pupa bears even less resemblance to the creature that creeps out of it one fine day. Three miracles must occur to create a butterfly. Just look here through the magnifying glass at this brown, cylindrical, unprepossessing piece of wood of a larva, and then regard the minute scales on the wings, stardust, no other living creature bears comparison. A butterfly is a rainbow of flesh and blood, not merely an optical illusion in the sky, it is something we will never understand.

We were four brothers who had all, at one time or another, posed my father variations on the question of what the sense was in our researching something which, after all, defied comprehension. I remember my father's triumphant smile when he answered: "What is more interesting than the incomprehensible? The day everything lies open to our eyes, we will simply turn our back and start on something even more incomprehensible, only *that* makes sense."

He may have been paraphrasing Humboldt, or perhaps his friend

Alfred E. Brehm, author of *Brehm's Animal Life*. But I like to think they were his own words.

In addition to all the butterflies and beetles, we also captured many birds that summer and discovered a completely new species – a beautiful little woodpecker. It was later given the name Lyngipicus doerriesi, after us. I am almost certain it was the ornithologist Bolau who bestowed that honour upon us.

Between Askold and the mainland lie the so-called Unkowski stones, flat slabs of rock that the sea washes over when storms hit the coast. Through field glasses we could just discern the Asian ringed seals (*Pusa hisbida*) who galumph up out of the sea to rest on them. It was of course tempting to hunt them for both their skulls and their skins, objects that zoological museums would be delighted to have.

Jankovskij's small boat was not up to the task, but we were able to rent a curious vessel belonging to a Manchu, which lay along the shore to gather seaweed. The boat was fashioned out of the trunk of an enormous oak. I think the man had hollowed it out himself, all six and a half metres of it. We paid him a few roubles, climbed aboard, raised the sail and within an hour were out by the stones. We lowered the sail, crouched down, and let the tide carry us closer because seals are shy and disappear into the sea at the slightest disturbance.

The sea was calm that day, and we were about twenty metres away before all the heads visible turned in our direction, a total of eight animals. They could probably only make out the outline of the boat, for the corneas of a seal which has not been in the water for a time assume a dryness that impairs vision; as soon as the animal is submerged again their sight returns to normal.

We loaded our rifles, took aim and shot simultaneously, firing two bullets into the neck of the largest male. It threw itself around and plunged in the water, only to re-emerge quickly a moment later despite its injuries, probably with the intent of warning or locating the floating herd.

Meanwhile we had come within ten or twelve metres range. Henry put a bullet in its head and that settled the matter. Our beautiful prey was almost two metres in length and weighed almost one hundred and fifty kilos. Fortunately the last bullet had gone through the skull without leaving a large wound; the animal was wonderfully suited to preparation and became a very valuable object in our collection.

We wanted to spend autumn on the mainland and had arranged for the captain of a small schooner to come and pick us up on a specific date. But the boat did not arrive and our provisions were now all but used up. The gold wash works was inactive and unmanned, unfortunately, so we had to live off venison and pheasant for more than four weeks.

We grew thinner and thinner with each passing day, and were beginning to feel lightheaded and out of sorts. The human body is not designed to live on meat alone, although we made sure to consume some berries and withered herbs to avoid scurvy. But still there was no boat in sight.

We had to accept that our only way out was to attempt the unappealing voyage in the vessel we had borrowed for the seal hunt, and luckily the Manchu was still in the area. But he had serious misgivings about our idea, mostly due to the sudden storms that were now hitting the coast. Nevertheless, an offer of thirty-five roubles, to be paid on completion of a successful crossing, was enough to persuade him.

"Yes, I'm willing to risk my life for so *little*", he said dramatically, no doubt hoping we would pay him more.

So, in the hollowed-out tree trunk – without a keel! – we set out one morning at dawn in a choppy enough sea on the hazardous voyage. We had packed the sealed chests with our collections in watertight canvas and stowed these on the bottom of the deck, as well as tethering everything as securely as we could; should we capsize, at least the sodden craft would not sink.

The seaweed gatherer – he was, incidentally, a Chifu Manchurian and a passionate opium smoker – did not inspire me with confidence, so after an hour at sea I took over at the tiller. The swells grew more unsettled and the wind picked up. To our good fortune we had the wind behind us, and the floating trunk glided easily through the water, under a quarter of the sail, since we had to constantly reef.

At about eleven the next morning, a shark about six metres in length turned up to keep us company. It butted its head against the rudder and underside of the hull repeatedly and pursued us for a good five minutes. It was no doubt expecting something edible and I would have taken great pleasure in putting a bullet in its head but dismissed the idea for fear it might overturn the boat in its death throes.

In this hazardous manner the day passed.

Night fell and the waves grew in strength. Following each dip and surge of the sea, we found ourselves deluged and we were literally swimming within the boat. Henry and the Manchurian sat on the deck and had more than enough to do just bailing water. We were all soaked to the skin and frozen stiff. It was pitch black, neither moon nor stars were to be seen through the dense cloud.

We kept a constant eye out for Skreplov Lighthouse, without catching sight of anything at all, and around midnight I realised that we could not have put more than thirty sea miles behind us.

After three more nerve-racking hours, however, the lighthouse did turn up, visible in short tiny blinks at first, but at least we knew we were somewhat on the right course. When finally a low strip of light appeared in the east, we breathed a sigh of relief. It was not until about ten in the morning, however, that we could confirm we had survived and steer towards a rocky beach in Ussuri Bay.

Cold, wet and stiff, we went ashore and were fortunate to be given shelter by some Manchurian acquaintances of the seaweed gatherer in a cabin only a few hundred metres away. We were also given a little food, including the marvellous black bread we had been without for weeks. After a few hours of heavy slumber, we rented two small packhorses from our hosts. The seaweed gatherer accompanied us over the hills, and following a three-hour trek, we were back at Gammenthaler's tavern, where Fingauka and Leon were overjoyed to see us; they had grown fat and lazy during the summer and autumn, in contrast to us. In teeming rain, we managed to move the chests under cover and paid the Manchurian ten roubles more than we had agreed. He did not look best pleased as we bade him farewell.

29

The collection was dry, intact, and ready to be shipped to Europe. And we were well under way with that work when Gammenthaler mentioned that a Chinaman had visited the inn, about once a month for the past year, asking for me. He described the man and I realised it must have been my old friend Wanka.

Gammenthaler said he had seemed upset and had perhaps wanted money. I understood very little of this and resolved to look into it. But the following day we received a visit from my old friend Hoeck the whaler, who had once provided me with passage from Yokohama, and in the intervening period had also sold me several exquisite ethnographic objects from the Chukchi and Koryaks, the peoples on the Kamchatka Peninsula and by the Bering Strait.

But the reunion was anything but cheerful; Hoeck's face was ashen and haggard, and he had a terrible tale to tell: he owned a farm on the Sidimi Peninsula – that is to say, south of the regions we had been collecting in over the last few years – where, between his Arctic expeditions, he lived a sedate life with a wife and three children. Sometimes he had to sail to Vladivostok in the schooner to purchase supplies, and during his last absence a band of Chinese marauders, the imperishable Honghuzi yet again, had seized the opportunity to kill his wife, two of his children and two Russian workers. And they had done a thorough job: they had driven treenails under the poor woman's fingernails and toenails. Then they had carved her up and hanged her still alive from the ceiling over the parlour table. And the two children, aged three and five, had been cut up into pieces and placed on the table below her. There was no trace of the third child, a girl of seven. Hoeck could only assume she had fled into the sea and drowned.

I asked as to what he intended to do. And as if there were no other answer:

"Pursue the Honghuzi and kill them, every last one of them."

He was in the city now seeking assistance to that end. Naturally, Henry and I offered to accompany him, although I simply could not imagine – no matter how vengeance was exacted – how Hoeck could manage to go on living with the image of his massacred family in his mind.

The city governor placed twelve specially trained soldiers at our disposal.

So, postponing work on our shipments, we boarded Hoeck's schooner the next morning and a favourable wind saw us sailing south to Sidimi in less than five hours. Well stocked with provisions, weapons and ammunition, we wasted no time in mounting the horses to take up pursuit. Fingauka and Leon took up the front, the two layabouts now given a chance to exert themselves.

The tracks led south along the beaches but became unclear after a time. The dogs lost the scent, so Hoeck dispatched some soldiers up into the mountains, while the rest of our party continued along the coast.

We had criss-crossed the landscape for three days, and were nearing the frontier with Korea, when two scouts returned and reported a faint column of smoke coming from an area of brush a few hundred metres further on. We advanced cautiously and soon came to a dilapidated dwelling. As darkness was falling, Hoeck decided we would surround the building from a distance and attack at first light.

Our preparation was optimal. Our encirclement was most successful and the dogs remained as silent as if hunting gamebirds. In the grey light of dawn we moved through the brush towards the dwelling. The trees had lost their foliage, but the hazel shrubs retained their leaves far into winter, keeping us well hidden.

We had split into two groups, and as soon as we heard shots being fired from our other contingent we knew the dance could finally begin. Henry and I advanced at speed, firing what we had at the rogues we could spot as we ran. But old Hoeck – who was leading our group – suddenly came running in the opposite direction, his face bloodied, and asked me to check if his right eye was injured.

Fortunately it was not. A Honghuzi bullet had splintered the stock of his weapon, shattering his spectacles, and sending pieces of glass into his cheeks and forehead. I removed most of the shards, bandaged him hastily, and we re-joined the fray.

One Honghuzi popped up right in front of me, but before I had a chance to fire he took cover behind a birch tree. I too jumped behind a tree, a bullet hitting the trunk behind my head a moment later. I peeped around, catching sight of the rogue's left arm as he put in more ammunition, and managed to shoot him in the elbow. He kneeled down to complete reloading, a difficult task with the wound he had suffered, and I managed to put one more bullet in his right arm.

He flung his weapon away, ran to seek refuge in the brush behind and then I shot him a third time, in the back, and he fell down face forward. Considering what Hoeck's wife and children had been subjected to, being dispatched like this was hardly punishment enough.

According to the soldiers, seven men had made it through our positions south of the dwelling, but four of these were wounded. The dogs found a further two men, who were executed right away, as well as nine bodies. Two of the Russian soldiers had suffered minor wounds. One Honghuzi whom Captain Hoeck had shot through the jaw was granted release by a shot to the back of the head. Although not all of them had got what they deserved we had at least made a good job of thinning their ranks. In addition, we got hold of four Winchesters and six old Russian army rifles, along with a few daggers.

Thus ended those terrible few days.

We made camp, the soldiers brewed tea, ate, and talked about what had happened. The last reddish rays of sunlight played among the clouds and night began to fall. The hazy atmosphere drifted from the plains out over the sea, where the sporadic flash of playful fish could be seen. High above us wild geese flew, while I lay listening to the sound of the waves beneath the deep sky, dotted with stars, glorious and exalted. Moments like these can fill a person with reverence. This must be how it is in war, I thought, when the horror and the beauty merge to form some higher unity and the body quivers with a sensation that can only be experienced in close contact with death.

*

Winter was fast approaching and the bare trees stood looking lifeless – what had become of the splendid array of rich colours in Sidimi? But this season also had its charm, and as the southern part of the peninsula had yet to be scientifically explored, Henry decided to stay with Captain Hoeck and collect winter birds and animals, while I resolved to travel to Europe and make personal contact with the institutions that had received our objects over the years, an idea I had been entertaining for a while, due I think both to curiosity and the need to assure myself that everything was progressing as it should.

There were no sad farewells. Henry had always said that he would never return to Europe. He loved Siberia and had become, to all intents and purposes, a Russian. He spoke the language as though it were his mother tongue and could not imagine living anywhere else. And Hoeck could barely conceal his delight at the prospect of having company through the winter.

30

On October 20, 1884, we sailed into Vladivostok on board Hoeck's schooner, where after a short and hectic week, we had everything ready and I could go aboard the Russian steamer *Petersburg*, which was bound for Europe.

But at the very moment of departure I was to suffer a terrible blow. Fingauka was standing beside Leon next to Henry on the quay, unsettled and whimpering, and after the *Petersburg* set sail and was a couple of hundred metres from the shore, my four-legged friend tore away, jumped into the sea and began swimming after the boat. I could see Henry waving his arms about and shouting in desperation, it looked like Leon was going to jump in after him, while I myself ran back and forth on the aft deck, a helpless spectator to the drama. Fingauka swam and swam through the icy waters in the boat's wake. It was a terrible sight, the inexorable increase in distance between both the dog and the ship and between the dog and the shore, it looked like my friend was not moving at all, but was standing still, floundering in an undertow. I blinked, but no doubt kept my eyes closed for a little longer than necessary, because when I opened them there was only a flat expanse of sea to be seen between the ship and the figures on the quayside, who also soon vanished from view, first Leon, then Henry.

This affected me to such an extent that I barely ate before we reached the Strait of Malacca. Both the Indian Ocean and the Red Sea seemed even deader than the last time I had crossed them, as an excited 25-year-old. In the Bosporus, however, an incident occurred which put my mind on other matters.

As it was pitch dark when we arrived, the captain thought he could navigate into Constantinople without giving notification of our arrival. But the Turks had seen us from the fort, and as we gave no sign of stopping, they fired five warning shots, and not blanks across our bow, but cannonballs whistling over the deck. They would no doubt have sunk us if the captain had not immediately followed orders. But as soon as we anchored up, a smiling delegation came aboard, approved our papers, and wished us a pleasant onward journey.

This episode remains in my memory not only because it steered my thoughts away from the loss of a dog, but also because it was the first time I saw the famous Topkapi in Sultanahmet, illuminated like a palace from a children's book, the light so clear and bright that we thought it must be artificial, a curious observation, since electricity was in its infancy.

We continued up the Bosporus into the Black Sea and then headed for Odessa. On this stretch of the voyage I made a small sketch of Fingauka. I was not particularly pleased with the result, so perhaps the later loss of the drawing was meant to be. From Odessa I travelled by train to Hamburg, arriving home on Christmas Eve no less, to much rejoicing by the family, as I had come unannounced.

The work of selling the fruits of our labour proceeded satisfactorily, but there was a lot, and it took time. Fortunately the profits were better than expected. Everywhere I went I was met with goodwill and interest, procuring new requests and instructions, and after only a month was already planning my next expedition.

However, my father was so enthused by the impressive collections, and in particular everything I had to tell, that he insisted on accompanying me on my return and seeing the Siberian wilderness with his own eyes. Without mentioning it to mother or anyone else in the family he had already sought a leave of absence from his work as *futtermeister* at the city zoo.

This caused a terrible to-do. Mother was alive and well and now faced the prospect of not just three, but four of the men in her life more or less in peril on the far side of the world; our youngest brother, Edmund, was working in the Amazon at the time, and apparently the postal service was even worse there than in Siberia. Like Henry, Edmund had also set off on his travels aged just sixteen.

But father had not only dedicated his life to science and dispatched his sons on adventures in their teens, he also had a stubborn and wilful nature, so there was nothing for it but to give in to him.

We secured passage on a smallish steamer. And on April 24, 1885, we said our goodbyes to the family, gathered in their best attire on the quayside. We both found our cabins, and then proceeded up on deck to stand at the railing and wave, Mother despondent and teary-eyed, wearing an ample flowery dress under a large black shawl, as though in mourning, my sisters somewhat more collected, and giggling, and father shouting some final instructions down to them in a booming voice, about how to manage the house and property in his absence, watering the plants in the greenhouse, feeding the birds, dusting the stuffed animals that filled every nook and cranny of our home, we had practically grown up in a natural history museum.

But we had not even reached the open sea before the old fellow became seasick. It was no mild form of seasickness either, he was so poorly he wanted to die, and asked in a pleading voice if the entire journey would be as bad as this.

I suggested it would probably be slightly calmer in the Mediterranean, at least through the Suez canal. He realised the battle was lost and there was only one thing to do: I went up to the bridge to try and convince the captain – through financial incentive if necessary – to turn the boat around.

He was an agreeable man of a similar age to my father, and he smiled when I explained matters. But it was now further to Hamburg than to Dover, so we ended up sailing to England. I accompanied my father ashore and he cried like an infant as we embraced and took leave of one another.

I learned later that he soon found passage back to the continent, but was just as seasick on this journey, and had taken to his bed upon arrival home and not stirred from it for a month, after which he returned dejectedly to his work at the zoological garden.

31

I wanted my stay in Vladivostok to be as brief as possible, but I heard via Gammenthaler that the "Chinaman" had been around again asking for me.

I told him that Wanka was not Chinese but Manchurian, and he placed great importance on the distinction. Gammenthaler handed me a letter written in rather illegible Russian which I could only interpret as Wanka reproaching me for something or other, so I borrowed one of Gammenthaler's horses and went to visit my old friend at an address he had provided at the bottom of his missive, a small settlement outside the city. It appeared neat and tidy, what Russians call a dacha, with three small gardens, plots and a well-kept house. I knocked and Wanka appeared immediately. At first he was happy as a child to see me but then began to admonish me for travelling alone to Askold the previous year.

I told him I had gone with my brother, Henry.

It was precisely this that was such a disgrace; when one has gone through something important together with someone, then the two of you are brothers, so why had I chosen Henry?

I had to smile at this and replied that Henry was my own flesh and blood, whereupon Wanka began to tear his hair out and said that now

I had to accompany him in to meet his dying father and swear to him that he was a good man.

I was growing weary of all this but followed him obediently inside. The house bore clear traces of a woman's touch, but there was no woman to be seen – Wanka had four younger sisters – and in the innermost room lay a very elderly Manchurian with eyes closed in a hand-carved Russian wooden bed. He had a few wisps of hair on his head and his face was as smooth as a child's. Wanka woke him up with a gentle shake and said a few authoritative words – in Manchurian – and the old man looked up at me.

"Say it now!"

"What shall I say?"

I was to tell him that Wanka was a good son.

"But can your father understand Russian?"

"Yes, yes, of course. He believes I'm a stranger since I returned from my travels with you."

I could see the paradox, but did as instructed, telling the old man his son had been a blessing to me and that he was a capable, trustworthy man. He seemed to grasp the message and closed his eyes again, waving us away with a limp hand, and we left.

Nevertheless, as we stood in the little garden I had the impression that my testimony had failed to completely satisfy Wanka, or that during the séance he had found something new to ponder, like when we were in the field and I showed him something he had not noticed before. But finally he shook my hand, thanking me with tears in his eyes, and said things would no doubt go well for me – "you have your brother".

I left for the city straight away, sleeping a night at Gammenthaler's before securing what equipment and provisions I needed. Then it was back to Sidimi in a hulk of a Japanese fishing boat, which I would dearly have liked to have taken command over: the skipper was hopeless at his job, as bad as the fellow in charge of the junk that had got us to Askold by the skin of our teeth the previous year.

On July 2, I arrived on Sidimi and was reunited with both my dear brother and Captain Hoeck, both in good health, although Hoeck had aged considerably. Fortunately – as was customary for him at this time of year – he was in full swing with preparations for the summer's Arctic sea expedition.

Sadly, I learned that Leon the dog had also perished, just months after Fingauka drowned. Ironically, he had fallen prey to a tiger, the animal he feared more than anything. There was, however, no news of Hoeck's eldest daughter, the one who had probably run into the sea. And as far as I am aware he never found out what happened to her.

The material Henry had collected during the winter was already packed, and Hoeck was willing to take us up the River Suifun in his schooner to the foot of the Tigrovo Paid mountains, where we planned on spending the rest of the summer, the autumn and perhaps also the winter.

Among the crew was a Koryak, a man in his forties from the territory north of Kamchatka. He had, however, great difficulty in pronouncing his name, or rather nobody was able to understand the sounds he made whenever he introduced himself, which was curious, as he spoke passable Russian, so Hoeck had simply christened him Samuel.

Samuel was very skilled, a son of the wilderness whom Hoeck had for years used as a scout, advisor and interpreter in the north. But last year he had taken him home with him because Samuel wanted to see "the south", and Samuel had done nothing but regret it since.

Although the winter here resembled a proper winter, the "tropical" summer was unbearable (we recorded a temperature of twelve degrees that day). Samuel complained about sweating and being unable to sleep; he did not like the way the forests obstructed his view and could not abide something else that I understood had to do with mist, moisture or vapour. He had now divested himself of the three outer layers of leather he was wearing but did not think he could very well remove the last and parade around naked on deck. Henry had been on countless hunting trips with him in the course of winter and did not tire of poking fun at him for all this whining.

I became well acquainted with Samuel during the trip and asked him to procure what items he could from up north – cooking utensils, hunting implements, clothes, weapons, handicrafts – all of which would later be exhibited in Europe, I promised. I also promised to pay well, and Samuel agreed to this, he was proud of his people. We sealed the deal with a ritual and solemn handshake, as though to set it in stone. It turned out to be a very lucrative arrangement for both of us.

32

In Tigrovo we had to share a house with a woodsman named Zavyalov, who lived with his wife and two children in the larger half of a dilapidated log building, which had been placed at our disposal, again by some Cossacks, which meant that Henry and I had to work in the same room where we slept and ate, but we did not mind.

Between expeditions into the wilderness that summer I wrote an extensive report on all the butterflies we had captured, and an even more comprehensive one on bird life, sending the latter to both Bolau and Noack, in the hope of having it published. And my efforts were successful: *Die Vogelwelt von Ostsibirien*, with descriptions of the 133 different species we had hitherto captured and/or observed.

Autumn was once again brief and dramatic, and an extremely harsh winter followed. By the end of October the thermometer already displayed fifteen below zero. And as beautiful as the landscape in eastern Siberia can be in spring, as bright as it can be in the summer and autumn, the days in November and December can appear just as fear-inspiring. The *purga* – the bitterly cold winter wind, sometimes whipping up a fine blizzard of snow – howls through the woods and across the steppes, boring into the skin and eyes. One snowstorm following the other, the forests seething in ceaseless wind, frost making dead trees crack so loudly one could imagine they had come back to life. The sun barely discernible, encircled by white rings. And it was just such a *purga* we fell foul of one day when we were hunting in the taiga, together for once, to our good fortune, but far from the log house.

Evening had fallen, and the storm simply prevented us from moving any further. We tried to light a fire while the wind whistled and howled, but had to give up. After shovelling the snow out from beneath an old Swiss pine, we settled in, where no-one would have found us, and were completely covered in the course of the night.

When dawn broke, we dug ourselves back out of the snowdrifts, ate a handful of snow to slake our thirst, and despite the ongoing storm, continued on our way, mostly to try to warm ourselves up again. The compass was all we had to cling on to, but a compass is meagre comfort when visibility is down to two or three metres, so we were forced to give up again, seeking shelter in a narrow ravine and allowing ourselves to be snowed under anew.

After yet another night we were utterly exhausted. But then the storm finally eased off and eventually on the evening of that third day we managed to make it home, spent and starving, with frostbite on our faces, hands and feet. And never had a snowed-over log house in the most desolate of wildernesses been a greater blessing. A snowstorm like the one we endured usually lasts for four days, this had only persisted for two.

33

We lived, as I mentioned, under the same roof as the woodsman Zavyalov. And the man absolutely gave the impression of being a released prisoner: he was strikingly tall and thin, his face was bony, his eyes fearfully dark, both piercing and evasive. Over pouting lips hung an ungroomed, brown moustache. He was probably about forty years old. And it was not long before we noticed he was a so-called "quarterly drinker", which was to say that around every third month he went into Vladivostok to purchase a forty-litre drum of 85% spirits.

As soon as he returned, he lay down in bed and washed the spirits down with a few gulps of water. And during periods like this he drank nothing else, nor ate or worked, to the great despair of the family. There was one occasion when the usual forty litres did not suffice and he apparently lacked the funds for a new supply. I was busy skinning a small brown bear on the living room floor when the door burst open and the Russian stumbled in. He had been without spirits for two days, he yelled, the thirst was driving him out of his mind. He knew we had some glass jars with snakes we had caught (*Vipera berus*) and preserved in alcohol, and he begged to have just one of them.

Having no desire to appear unsympathetic, I unscrewed the top of one and told him to help himself. He grabbed the jar, closed his eyes and let the precious fluid – now reddish-brown from the preservation process – trickle down his throat. After which he left without saying a word.

Perhaps a quarter of an hour or twenty minutes had passed, when a terrible racket erupted from his part of the house. Initially I paid no heed, but upon hearing gunshots I ran to the window. About one hundred metres away I saw his wife and children fleeing in panic towards the forest while Zavyalov stood swaying on the porch firing after them with a rifle. The Lord God must have had his hand upon them, because none of them were hit.

Some weeks later I had to travel to Vladivostok myself to stock up on food and ammunition; Henry rarely left the woods voluntarily. In the city I lodged as usual at Gammenthaler's and fell into conversation with some Russian hunters who were also staying there, and it turned out they knew Zavyalov, and he had indeed been a prisoner, but had not been released and was in fact a fugitive from a katorga on the penal island of Sakhalin. Naturally I became concerned for Henry, who was alone back at the house. But when I had eventually taken care of all my errands and returned, I found him safe and sound.

Much later, I found out that Zavyalov had persisted with murder and robbery for several years. A group of Chinese had, for a small fee, been granted permission by the Russian state to dig pitfalls in the forests around Tigrovo. It was deer antlers they were after. And one day one of them had passed the log house with a batch of antlers on his way to the city to sell them.

As this was the only bastion of civilisation along the stretch of road, he had gone in and asked for some tea. While enjoying Zavyalov's hospitality, he had proudly shown him a few antlers, and the Russian had offered him twenty roubles for them. The Chinese, aware he would get a better price in town, naturally did not want to sell and went on his way. But Zavyalov followed after, shot him, burned the body, and stole the antlers.

Over the course of six years he killed no fewer than twenty-two Chinese in this way. This was what he lived off: it all came to light one day, the logging was merely a façade.

Several years later I also got to hear how the Chinese had finally managed to do away with him, and in how curious a manner: in the village of Razdolni, about twenty kilometres from Tigrovo, some Chinese were in the process of building a bridge over a stream when Zavyalov drove up in a horse and cart, quite inebriated. As usual he managed to start an argument. But one of the Chinese, who had lost a brother at the Russian's hands, recognised him and informed his companions. On an appointed signal they all attacked him and did their best to trample him to death with their wooden shoes.

Some Russian farmers came on the scene and intervened, dragging the mutilated man to a farmhouse nearby and laying him on the floor. Close to death, Zavyalov begged that a priest be called so he could unburden his conscience before he breathed his last. His wish was granted, the priest arrived, Zavyalov made his confession, and the priest managed in his wisdom to forgive the murderer all his sins, before he died in great pain.

34

A hundred paces into the woods, to the east of the house in Tigrovo, a gigantic Linden tree grew; as perfect a tree as I have seen in my life, a Tilia mandshurica, more than forty metres high and more than two metres in diameter when measured a metre and a half above the ground. I calculated it to be in the region of eight hundred years old, hence far older than the famous Linner Linden in Switzerland.

But it was neither its size nor age that made this tree unique, but its personality: the forty or fifty branches furthest down were inclined downwards to the earth and had over hundreds of years become covered in falling leaves and grass which had turned to soil. These branches now extended down into the root system, and in the cavity beneath them eternal night reigned, wherein not a flake of snow nor a drop of rain ever penetrated. From a distance the tree looked like it was standing atop a bell-shaped hill; only from close range could one see that the hill was in fact the lower branches of the tree. I paced out a distance of two hundred and twenty steps walking around this marvel.

Right from the start we thought there was something magical about it. And with my love for trees I could not help but think of a huge oak I had had outside my bedroom window when I worked as a horticulturist in Lübeck – it was approximately two thousand years old, thus the same age as the olive trees in Gethsemane, which had witnessed Jesus's wanderings. But the Lübeck oak was nearly dead, only two small branches on the black skeleton still bore leaves, and I envisioned all of Germany's history in that moribund giant, from the savage wilderness that was the Teutoburg Forest to the neat and peaceful park now surrounding it.

Our Linden tree in Suifun, on the other hand, was full of life, and told us each morning what type of weather it was, where the wind was coming from, how strong it was and how heavily the rain was falling. By its silence we also imagined it could report how lightly or heavily the snow was falling.

One summer's day I was alone at home working on packing butterflies when I heard a low whimper coming from the tree and went closer to investigate. We had carefully cut away some of the bottom branches to make it possible to enter the magical space beneath them. And in the darkness within I came across a deer lying on its stomach, with forelegs pointing in my direction, like an obedient dog before its master. I kneeled down to allow more light to pass over my shoulders, and we stayed there looking at one another. The deer remained quite calm, but was trembling.

Then I discovered it had a bullet wound to its back. It was fresh and bleeding profusely, and several vertebrae were broken. I returned to the house to fetch the rifle and put the poor animal out of its misery. Later, I was in the process of quartering the deer when Henry arrived home, looking rather down in the mouth, but would not say what was bothering him. Noticing the deer, he asked if I had also been out. I said no, and he admitted to having wounded a deer about five or six versts to the south-west. We realised it had to have been the same animal and began examining the offal. And we found the bullet, the same ammunition as we used. So how had the wounded deer managed to drag himself all the way here? And why seek refuge to die under *our* tree of all places?

35

As a collector is not always armed, it is important to exercise caution when one is in areas with many brown and Asian black bears. One day I heard Henry's new Golde dog begin to bark – they were working on a slope approximately two hundred metres uphill from me. The barking grew fiercer and fiercer and then I heard an incoherent scream from my brother. The next moment he came stumbling out of the brush, bleeding profusely from several wounds with his right arm dislocated.

A Tibetan she-bear (Asian black bear) with cubs had launched a vicious attack on him. But the dog had counter-attacked and not given up until the powerful beast had let go of its prey and quit the scene.

After I had bandaged the poor fellow, he managed to stagger back to the house under his own steam, from where I brought him by wagon to the German hospital in Vladivostok, which we reached around midnight the following day. He was in the best of hands there, so somewhat reassured I returned to the house.

A few days later, I encountered a none too pleasant rival of this Asian black bear, yet another keen insect collector, when an enormous bear rose up only five metres in front of me, Herr Ursus arctos v. behringiana in person, Asia's largest species. We appeared to be heading in the same direction, and as I was again unarmed – and had Henry's experience fresh in my mind – I kept as calm as possible and allowed the bear go ahead of me, almost bowing as it passed. The one-and-a-half-metre beast growled a couple of times and lumbered casually away in the direction it had apparently intended.

And I could then avail myself of the old trusty method, and began to wander behind the bear at a distance of about a hundred paces, using the net to scoop up the insects it flushed out. We continued like this until late at night, moving upwind all the time, and I saw no sign that the animal felt it was being stalked.

But then it came to a halt by a huge windthrow, an elm with a split running from the crown to the root system, probably the result of a light-ning strike, completely overgrown by moss and scrub. Out of the blue the bear began to attack it, running around and sniffing at it, sinking its claws in the rootstock and pulling with all its strength, although it was unable to budge the giant tree.

Then it set about the crown, breaking off – one by one – the branches lying on the ground, which the bear probably understood was the reason the tree could not be moved. I had never seen the like. With its tremen-dous strength, it finally managed to overturn the fifty-foot-long trunk, issued a growl of satisfaction, and began pawing at the moist soil for the grubs, mice and insects that immediately came to light.

When Henry returned, with a considerable number of surgical stitches in both his face and on his body, and one arm in a sling, I gave my report on the successful cooperation with the behringiana, and he was left unamused. But when I related the details of the bear's assault on the elm tree his mood lightened, although it did take more than a week before he could fire a shot again, or lift the net. And it was a relief to see him avoid the same fate as Gavrilov, the Cossack who had come face to face with a bear and not only suffered grievous injury to his body, but also to his mind.

One night in June we were preparing a butterfly haul, which is to say we were packing the animals with their wings almost folded into cone-like, waxed paper bags before placing them tightly together in small wooden boxes, which were then stacked in larger boxes and subsequently packed into chests and sealed.

We logged all the specimens, the time they were captured, the date, the location (indicated on a map), a description of the species (to the extent we were able to determine it), local vegetation, meteorological conditions like humidity, precipitation, temperature. It was painstaking and rewarding work, as any collector will attest to. Gazing down at these wings tightly packed together can only be compared to admiring the pages of an illuminated gospel. It is therefore with a feeling of slight sorrow but great triumph that one seals the lid of such a chest, knowing that from now on the treasures are in Father's hands, thereafter in Otto Staudinger's, for thorough examination, before they can eventually be exhibited to the European public. This is the collector's most uplifting thought, his life's purpose.

In the middle of this work, however, a Russian hunter aged about sixty arrived, quite out of breath. He told us that an hour's walk from the house he had wounded a she-tiger who had been lying on a fallen tree trunk, proudly watching over her cubs:

"I fired off a shot. And hit the target too, but she dropped from the tree trunk and vanished into the brush, and I didn't dare venture in there. I fired a couple more shots but I don't think I hit."

I asked the old hunter, who claimed he had killed more than twenty tigers in the course of his life, to show us the upturned tree, and to stay in the background.

It is worth pointing out that tracking a wounded she-tiger in summertime, when visibility is limited, is extremely demanding and rarely does any good come of it. Furthermore, a wounded tiger will move in cunning loops when being followed, will stay low, hugging the ground, and attempt to overpower the pursuer.

But we were tempted by the valuable hide, and the animal was wounded.

By the fallen tree we soon found tracks which led us to marshy terrain where the reeds grew above eye level. Here and there we saw drops of blood on the stems, leading us to think that perhaps she had been shot in the stomach. But the visibility grew poorer and poorer, so we crept on our knees through the boggy water, in order to at least see a metre or two in front of us, under the foliage. And by a small stream we suddenly caught sight of the animal, perhaps twelve or thirteen paces away, sitting on the ground like a dog. She had heard us long ago and now lifted her head to stare as us with keen eyes. We could not afford to hesitate – our shots rang out at the same time, and the cat sprang immediately in our direction, but to no avail. The beautiful creature collapsed, dying a few metres from us.

It turned out the bullet from the old hunter had lodged in the animal's spine.

We had left the dog at home – this one was also terrified of tigers – and in addition a terrible thunderstorm broke out, so we ended up not searching for the lair and the cubs; when a wounded she-tiger feels she is unable to look after her young she will chase them away. I have seen similar behaviour in other predators and in prey, deer mothers are known to resort to it.

In the middle of the most astonishing downpour, we removed the fur of the feline. The old Russian received ten roubles, as well as the bones, which the Chinese pay a good price for, and in their naivety use as medicine.

But in spite of the success of the hunt, we were, in the torrential rain, struck by that heavy feeling which can sometimes overcome a hunter when he has torn such a perfect creature out of existence, a feeling only intensified by our knowledge of how much devotion maternal predators display in nurturing and caring for their young. And we never found the two tiger cubs. We even looked under the enormous linden tree, but they were not to be found anywhere.

36

In late summer, we said goodbye to Tigrovo and the linden tree, and travelled by horse and wagon south towards Sidimi, reaching Hoeck's farm on August 30, 1887.

Gale-force winds had blown from the north-west for the entirety of our journey, increasing on the night of our arrival to storm force, and subsequently to a hurricane. Anything not tied up on the beach was swept away by the breakers. A Korean vessel at anchor in the ordinarily well-sheltered bay was dashed to pieces against the rocks. Two crew members were killed, and the remainder suffered serious injuries. We picked up the ones we found, got them indoors and dressed their wounds to the best of our abilities. A bridge that Hoeck had built over the little river nearby that flows into the sea was also swept away.

After a few days the wind abated and the sea stilled, and we could load our chests aboard Hoeck's schooner. We were also pleased to discover that our friend Samuel the Koryak had sent a magnificent collection of objects from his people up north: fetishes and a variety of amulets, jewellery carved from whale and walrus teeth, cradles, a sled with runners made of walrus tusks, spears, arrows, harpoons, clothes of reindeer hide and seal skin, as well as some hunting traps. This precious collection was later sold to the Museum of Ethnology and was at the centre of an amusing incident which I shall return to.

Hoeck brought us to Vladivostok, where we spent a few days at Gammenthaler's rooms, but wanted to waste no more time than strictly necessary getting back to the Bikin, the mightiest tributary of the Ussuri, in many regards the most important area we mapped in the course of our activity in Siberia, with a unique interplay between natives, wild animals and the land that I cannot extol highly enough.

We travelled north by horse and wagon to the village of Kirovsky by the banks of the Ussuri. There we went aboard a river steamer that carried us downriver to the Cossack village of Kozlovska, at the mouth of the Bikin, spending some time there to pick out four almost fully-grown Golde dogs. We bought a riverboat, loaded the dogs and equipment aboard, paddled upstream, and three days later arrived back at our old log cabin.

It was somewhat overgrown, and the old sleigh needed repairing, but we had tools with us as usual, so that only took a few days. We had a multitude of provisions, mostly black bread, tea, sugar and salt, as well as enough weapons and ammunition and what was required of other equipment. We got meat from the forests and fat from bears and wild boar. The Bikin is surrounded by low hills cut by transverse gorges and small valleys, and in the summer months the river provided us with all the fish we needed.

Not more than a few hundred metres from our log cabin, a settler by the name of Fyodor Paskevich had recultivated the land on the old settlement and established himself along with a wife and three daughters, aged six, three and two. They had come from a small town west of the Urals. The hay was already stacked, and according to his wife, Fyodor had just left to go hunting.

After fixing up the cabin for a while, we also set out. I came across a herd of deer, managed to shoot the largest buck, threw it over my shoulders and headed homeward.

When I was almost there, the wife of the Cossack and the eldest daughter suddenly appeared from behind one of the haystacks, both distraught and in tears. I asked what was going on and they pleaded with me to chase off some Honghuzi who had forced their way into the house and threatened them at knifepoint. They now feared the worst for the younger children, who were still inside with the criminals.

I threw down the deer and ran as fast I could up towards the farm to see off the scum. But they must have seen me, because as I rounded the corner of the house, I saw three men vanish into the forest. I fired a few shots after them, then walked back to the farm expecting to find a similar bloodbath to what Hoeck had experienced on Sidimi. But the youngest girl was sitting inside playing on the floor quietly with a hare made of straw, whilst her older sister was standing at the window, weeping, and looking for her mother.

I ran back down to the distraught woman, who was still hiding behind the haystack, and told her that the children were fine. She sank to her knees, her face a mixture of sorrow and joy, blessed herself and mumbled a quick prayer. We went back up to the house together. She hugged the children tightly, and more than a few tears were shed. I mixed her a stiff drink of spirits, water and a little sugar, which she knocked back in one. The nightmare was over. I searched the woods afterwards with one of the dogs, but found no trace or trail of blood anywhere, so my bullets had likely not hit anyone, which was fair enough, I thought.

37

One morning in September, I went out as usual to record the temperature for the log and found it showing minus eight degrees. The smaller lakes were thinly frozen over. A few tardy ducks landed on one pond but found no water, only mirror-still ice under their webbed feet. They stumbled around on the slippery surface for a while before taking flight again and continuing south.

Our dump of offal had as usual attracted winter birds, our most frequent guest being the coal tit (*Parus ater*), but we also recorded many long-tailed tit (*Parus caudatus*) and nuthatch, with the latter growing more and more tame. Soon we had three specimens living together with us, an amusing bird, full of trust. Oddly, a member of the far more timid goldcrest (*Regulus cristatus*) joined our company indoors. The tiny hummingbird-like creature fluttered around like a moth and could perch on the rim of my tea glass, and peck at breadcrumbs when it did not find grubs, spiders or insects in the timbered walls or under the roof boards, where it also slept.

Scarcely a month later, the main channel of the Bikin froze over, slow-moving as it is here. As mentioned, the Goldes live in this region, while the Orochs are to be found a little higher up, and the Museum of Ethnology in Hamburg were so pleased with the pieces we had sent them that they wanted more. With our dogs now trained to pull the sleigh, we set the birds free and started off up the frozen river.

We had great success on this trip as well, filling two chests with old, valuable objects which we managed to purchase or wangle from the Golde people, including some very rare tools, which we had not seen before, and even more variants of the old cradles passed down from generation to generation.

Of all the Mongolian peoples by the Amur and Ussuri rivers, the Gilyaks and the Goldes are the ones who have best managed to maintain their traditional way of life, in addition perhaps to the Udege people, who eke out an existence even higher up the valley, but we never made contact with them unfortunately.

Judging by the many stone implements still in use by both the Goldes and the Orochs, we surmised that these tribes must have inhabited the area for several thousand years. We also put all the tools they gave us to the test, and they were in no way inferior to the ones we ourselves used, quite the contrary.

Our visit also coincided with the annual bear festival: a young bear is caught in the spring, caged, and fed to be fat and virile. When the party starts, it is released and tries of course to flee to the woods but is mercilessly chased down by three or four Goldes who promptly plunge their *gida* spears into the poor creature, the whole thing accompanied by much whooping and screaming.

The blood and entrails are sacrificed to kindly disposed gods, while the meat and fat is consumed by the revellers, usually the entire village.

Spirits (*hauchen*), served hot, also play a central role. At night the young men dance around a bonfire until they pass out from exhaustion, and the following morning barely an inhabitant can remember what they did.

Fattened dogs are also slaughtered and made use of in the kitchen. We partook of the dish with our friends, but truth be told a sample taste was enough. Europeans in general find dog meat revolting, but particularly so when, as here, it is fried in fish fat. The Goldes also keep small, black pigs, which they fed solely on fish, and these are as inedible as the dogs.

38

In winter, one truly gains an insight into the hardships these people undergo, and the mystery of how they endure. The men had been hunting continuously for five days in the pine-covered highlands around the village, where in addition to deer and wild boar, there was also sable to be found, the most valuable of all animals. But the hunt on this occasion was unsuccessful. All they could do was trudge, tired and hungry, back down into the valley. The meat and fish stores were empty, the last dog had been butchered, and of course it pained a father to return empty-handed after such a slog and see his children sitting hungry round the fire. Everyone looking up at him, nobody saying anything, the infant sucking on a piece of leather, and the famished mother turning her back without uttering a word. We were witness to several such scenes.

About a week later – it was thirty-nine below freezing that morning, the air quivering with transparent frost – I noticed a young Golde woman leaving the village and disappearing into the woods with a bundle under her arm. I was already dressed for hunting, so I followed her until she came to a small clearing and dropped the bundle to the snowy ground. She then cut five or six hazel rods, arranged them in a ring and placed a deerskin over them. Finally, she dug out a little wood from under the snow, and soon a little fire was burning between the rods.

I approached and asked what she was doing out here on a day such as this?

She replied that she had sinned and had therefore to give birth to her child outdoors. She gave me to understand that there was nothing I could do, so I wished her well and left to hunt as planned.

Five days later I saw her again, staggering into the village and into her *fanse* bearing a tiny, living bundle in her arms, then sinking down exhausted on the *naren*, only to be greeted with the same indifferent fatalism that met the men when they returned empty-handed from the hunt, as though the entire tribe were saying *c'est la vie*. Both mother and child survived, however. It was a boy.

I should also mention that for many of these ethnic groups, children under a year old are not viewed as people but as birds, and should they die prior to their first birthday, an armband of sorts is drawn around their wrist with a piece of coal, so the soul can migrate into another woman. If a similar mark is discovered on a newborn child, it is considered reborn. An infant is a bird which cannot die.

I also received an insight into how the Goldes hunt, and what not using a firearm involved. The day began when, taking a break from preparing, I was standing outside smoking my pipe in the feeble rays of sunlight making a vain attempt to sow hope in the winter. Outside a *fanse* on the other side of a frozen stream, five Goldes were busy sharpening their spears with much clamour and laughter, as though preparing for a party.

I walked over and asked if they intended to go hunting.

They laughed and would not answer my question.

"You are all no doubt off to hunt tiger," I said, in jest, knowing all too well that they never hunt tiger, it is their sacred animal, the lord of the forest, whom they call *Marain*, it is a crime to kill a tiger. And they laughed even louder.

"A deer hunt, then?" I suggested. They were silent for a moment, then after some mumbling between themselves, the oldest in their party asked if I would like to come along. If I could credit them with any sense of irony, I would probably have interpreted this as the point where he thought it time to teach the German amateurs a lesson. Nevertheless, I chose to take him at his word and went to fetch my snowshoes and my own *gida* spear but left the rifle behind.

And we set off, six of us, but without dogs, which were useless in the deep snow, up to four feet deep in places. The Golde hunters trotted off unperturbed, however, while the oldest man informed me that they were now tired of fish, having not eaten anything else since the ice broke on the Bikin last spring, and it was time for some meat.

We soon found the tracks of a deer, quite a large one by the looks of them. But now it needed to be hunted down and corralled within spear range. This was no easy task, our prey had to be worn out. We ran, walked and crawled after the tracks, and I and the youngest man in our party, more of a boy really, were soon lagging behind. Fortunately, we could follow the trail of snowshoes, which crossed back on themselves several times in the course of the day, but only late at night did we manage to catch up with the hunting party. By that stage they had managed to kill the animal, a magnificent twelve-pointer, which lay steaming and bloody in the snow, penetrated by four spears. We gralloched it, and it turned out some internal organs had burst, so I presumed the meat was tainted, but they were unconcerned by this.

The carcass was carved up and distributed into four sacks. Then it was back to the settlement. When we finally arrived in the early hours of the morning, I was as drained of energy as I have only ever been on one other occasion. And the following day I did not venture out but lay indoors like an invalid while Henry teased and poked fun at me. Tragically, the youth was found dead in his *naren*, his lungs must have ruptured in the terrible cold. But this fatality was also viewed as one of existence's natural turns of fate. And venison was served at his funeral.

The Museum of Ethnology had tasked us with collecting skulls from the various indigenous tribes, an unpleasant as well as perilous assignment. We were only successful on two occasions.

Henry and I had been hunting a wolf for days along the Bira, yet another tributary of the Amur, and were quite worn out when we came upon a remote Oroch settlement and asked for shelter for the night. We were invited in and saw a shaman and his assistant in full swing, attempting to revive a terminally ill man of about forty without any hair. As usual, the shaman's arts yielded no fruit and the patient died before midnight. The following morning, the body was sewn into birchbark, whereupon his closest relatives carried it into the woods and placed it upon two suitable branches about eight feet above the ground. We accompanied the funeral procession and made a note of the spot, even though the freezing winter temperatures prevented the process of decomposition, and we could not do anything for the time being.

But in late summer the following year, after the flies and maggots had done their bit, we paddled into some reeds downstream from the spot, hid the boat and moved in the direction of the last resting place while catching moths.

The bark around the body was partially rotted away, and although the head was still attached by some tough sinews, with a bit of effort we managed to get it loose and bag it. We went back to the boat and paddled back downstream as quickly as possible. Thus, we carried out a task that, while unpleasant to us, was valuable to science.

In the summer, the Oroch and the Golde peoples fish also during the night, moving upriver on one of the minor tributaries with a metal plate mounted on the prow of the boat. They light a fire on this when darkness falls, and armed with harpoons, they let the current carry them downriver. The light from the fire reveals the location of the fish – one well-aimed thrust and the catch is speared and pulled into the boat.

But sometimes the fish does not end up in the boat, but rather the harpoon in the water, and it was on just such an occasion that a Golde also fell into the river and drowned. His friends pulled his body from the water, paddled to shore, dug a hole on the riverbank, and buried him with the usual ceremony, covering the grave with stones. They then placed a stick between the stones. We heard about the grave from a Cossack and later located it when we reconnoitred the area in daylight.

The following night we punted upriver on the Ussuri in gleaming moonlight. After a tiring two-hour journey, we steered into the Khor, arriving at the grave around midnight. We cleared the stones carefully away and found the skull. Some rats whose meal we had disturbed ran over our hands. This skull, like the other, was now held in place by sinews and had to be practically "screwed" off.

When we were back down by the riverbank and were busy washing the skull clean, two dogs turned up out of nowhere, both with bells around their necks, a hunting method we were both familiar with and had employed ourselves on several occasions: the Golde hunters move along the river by boat, keeping pace with the dogs, who, when they find prey on the bank, shake their heads gently to sound the bells, alerting the Goldes so they may paddle in and pick it up.

Although the skull was safely inside a sack, our proximity to the grave still made us feel uncomfortable. Nonetheless, we got away, unseen, or so we believed, but the theft was later discovered and created quite a stir. So, wishing to avoid any unpleasantness we punted back upriver and put the skull back in place.

Three days later I was called in for questioning by the local Cossack police. The Golde who had lodged the complaint called me a barbarian and asked what we had intended to do with the skull. I told him truthfully that skulls were exhibited in museums throughout Europe, that it was important to the advancement of knowledge and science, adding that the skulls of white men were also on show, and that those of men, women and children were to be found in every single institute of medicine.

At this the Cossack also seemed to lose all faith in civilisation. Whereupon I hastened to assure them that we had in this case merely taken some measurements of the skull and that it had been placed back with the body some time ago. But even this did not seem to serve to make them happier. However, after some bureaucratic dawdling the case was declared closed, and I was able to leave the interview as a free man. The following spring, we made our way upriver anew and fetched the skull for a second time, and this time it made its way to Europe with us.

39

On the morning of January 5, a Golde, in a state of some distress, entered the *fanse* we had borrowed, lamenting the loss of his best hunting dog to a tiger. Since the tiger is, as previously mentioned, a sacred animal it is strictly forbidden to hunt, he asked us to kill it for him.

Equipped with weapons and sufficient ammunition, we clambered onto the sleigh. After three-quarters of an hour on the river ice we came to the Golde's dwelling, where we ate and warmed ourselves up before setting out in pursuit of the animal.

At a bend in the river just upstream we found the spot where the tiger had crossed the ice and could also see tracks disappearing into the hazel bushes on the other side. The bravest of our dogs took up the scent immediately and was on its way towards the bushes when the tiger leaped out, pounced three metres through the air, killed the dog with a single swat, and dragged it back into the vegetation.

Our view was limited, so I fired off a warning shot. It had the effect however of causing some leaves to fall, and this was probably the reason the tiger re-appeared on the riverbank – and that was our moment. Both our bullets went through the animal's throat, and he died with our dog in his mouth.

We buried the dog in the snow. Our friend was extremely happy with the outcome, giving us some old, precious fetishes to show his appreciation, as well as lending us a sleigh to transport the animal on. After a three-hour trip downstream on the ice, we were back at the settlement.

While we were skinning the big cat that same night, some other Goldes turned up, sable hunters who asked if they could warm themselves in the *fanse*, and of course we invited them in. But no sooner had they caught sight of the tiger than they exited hurriedly again, because their fetishes – the *oetzicho* – had been exposed to the tiger and were therefore rendered useless. The *oetzicho* is essential to a sable hunt and is carried in the belt, wrapped in bearskin, so it will not be cold.

Once outside the tent, they tore off these now worthless objects, stamping contemptuously down on them in the snow and pronouncing some loud incantations before departing in great haste. Thus, our ethnographic collection was further enhanced by the addition of another ten items, which would otherwise have proved almost impossible to acquire. As far as I recall, the tiger's cranium and skin, along with the hides of some other predators, went to the museum in Leipzig.

The Amur tiger is undoubtedly of a calmer disposition than its counterparts in the jungles of India and on the Indonesian islands. But the eastern Siberian species can take hunting dogs right from under the nose of a hunter, and I have also seen it break into barns, killing both cows and horses.

At a smaller settlement one summer, we were witness to a tiger taking a foal, simply by sinking its teeth into the newborn creature's throat and jumping up onto a two-and-a-half-metre-high fence. Though it was dark,

I could see from an open window how the mighty beast made a supple turn atop the fence and tossed the foal over in a smooth parabola. As I could hear men's voices, I did not dare open fire. When the foal landed on the other side, the tiger jumped soundlessly down after it, took its prey in his mouth again and disappeared into the forest.

The next morning, the owner of the foal and four Cossacks got ready to go on a tiger hunt, two of them armed with rifles, the others with manure forks. Henry and I accompanied them and soon tracked down the thief. When the first bullets hit him – unfortunately missing any vital organs – it threw itself at the closest shooter. We reloaded and fired everything we had, eventually finishing the animal off. But only by exceptional efforts was the life of the badly maimed man saved. As far as I know he never made a full recovery, due in part to mental disturbance, which often affects individuals mauled by large predators.

One winter, a time when we had very little meat, I planned on hunting in a remote, mountainous area, so I left at five in the morning, while there was still moonlight. I had made the same trip the day before, without luck, and could now walk in my own snowshoe tracks. At one point, my dog made five or six evasive leaps to the side and soon after I discovered tiger tracks. And not only that: the animal had lain there the previous night, that was plain from the tracks, and had probably planned on taking my dog. But as the dog had been on my left side and the tiger lay in the thicket on the right, perhaps it had considered it too bold a move?

In the afternoon I managed to shoot an old stag.

I placed the liver and a leg in my backpack and buried the rest of the animal. The sun had already gone down, so I hurried out of the taiga.

On my descent I walked along a ridge with deep hollows on either side. And the dog drew again to a halt. Once more I discovered fresh tiger tracks, going in the same direction we were heading, which meant that for a time we had been moving parallel to the animals, at a distance of no more than ten to fifteen paces, while remaining blissfully unaware. The tigers had probably kept an eye on us the entire time. Judging by the tracks it was an adult female and a four-year-old cub. From this I concluded that even a tiger will give a human a wide berth if possible.

In any event it was now too dark to shoot, so the only option was to continue homeward. With a heavy heart, I arrived at the cabin, where Henry told me he had been plagued by strange, frightening premonitions. It was completely unlike him, he was sweating and had a desperate look in his eyes.

"I truly believed this would be your last hunt."

I asked if he had become superstitious. He replied that he had not and soon settled down. I told him about the tigers, and we agreed that though we did not believe in miracles, we had experienced many.

The tiger is not only perfectly adapted to its natural surroundings, like the butterfly, but also lives within the imagination of man, as both threatening and fascinating; admired, feared, hated and respected; no other animal is more talked about in Siberia, most often in reverential tones; no other animal has such an aura about it.

One afternoon, after a summery wagon ride from Suifun, we stumbled, hungry and tired, into a station to get food and fresh horses. During the meal we sat talking to the people living in the house and another traveller who said he was a vodka producer. He finished eating, paid, and bade us farewell. Shortly after, we also hitched up our horses and set off ourselves, and in the open landscape we were able to keep an eye on the wagon in front, even though it was four or five hundred metres ahead. The three horses pulling it were rounding a swing when a tiger suddenly pounced from the bushes, tore the nearest beast loose from the team, dragged it off the road, harness and all, and disappeared.

We cursed loudly that this occurrence had not befallen us, as we always had loaded guns at the ready when travelling by wagon.

We made it to the scene of the attack and took up pursuit, but even with a horse to lug, our quarry had either managed to hide or move faster than us.

On another journey, also by horse and wagon, but this time on my own, I stopped at a station where the manager related how the previous night his wagon had been attacked by a tiger, but with quite a different outcome: one of the horses had received slight injuries to its flank, and for some reason the tiger had given up and quietly withdrawn back into the forest.

The next morning, I drove to the spot specified, followed the tracks, and after just a kilometre, found the carcass of an elderly tiger that had obviously starved to death. On examination it turned out that one of its canines was missing, while the rest were worn halfway down. His claws were completely worn down and his body was emaciated. I skinned the animal, preparing both the hide and the skull sometime later. It was by no means a prize specimen, but I managed to sell it to an American whaler in Vladivostok for a remarkably good price, a tiger is after all a tiger, *marain*, the king of the forest.

40

In August and September, the salmon make their migration upriver, and the Oroch, Golde and Gilyak peoples catch them in large nets, thus securing an essential supply of food for the winter. And being so fond of fish as he is, the tiger also usually puts in an appearance along the riverbank, trying to snatch a salmon or two, even though he is far from as skilled in this endeavour as the bear.

It was at this time of year when, after just scaling a hundred-metre-high crag, I spotted a tiger on the bank below, peacefully consuming a salmon. I got in position, took aim and without hesitation placed a bullet between its shoulder blades. The beautiful beast jumped to its feet, did a somersault, and to my horror soared through the air, landing into deeper water to be swallowed up by the fast-moving current. After a minute or so it briefly appeared again, only to vanish from view for good; the craggy, rugged terrain rendered pursuit impossible. But the image of the tiger being carried along by the raging waters has stayed with me as a nagging memory of failure, of something unfinished, which I still return to in darker moments. I just do not like this memory, and yet it will not leave me, and that must assuredly mean something.

*

We also made interesting observations of how varied the behaviour could be even between animals of the same family. When the large rivers are frozen, the otter will travel overland to the forests at higher altitudes to winter by a river or stream still uncovered by ice. It moves in the snow like a seal in water, kicking its legs and sliding effectively and effortlessly several metres at a time, a joy to watch, and it is difficult to imagine an animal better formed for all elements: agile as a fish in water, swifter than a sable on land and superior to all other predators in the snow, all it lacks really are wings.

Then there is the otter's larger cousin, the badger, of which we also caught many. I once encountered a young male of the species, which my dog, much to its chagrin, was not able to get the better of, I had been alerted by its furious barking. The badger spun around quick as a flash when it saw me, growling and baring its teeth, acting on the whole in a very threatening manner, like the predator it is. But as I approached, it lowered its head and sought refuge between my legs, of all places. I had to yank at the lead to keep the dog at bay, and the badger peered up in confusion as though posing a question, before lowering its head again and lumbering quickly away towards its den, while I stood there too stunned to lift the rifle.

I have seen many animals run, and I am reluctant to call any of them laughable, all creatures are beautiful in their own way, but this mustelid ran – hopping, light as a feather, but almost sideways through the terrain – like a dust ball being pushed over a parlour floor. But in fairness, it managed to evade both hunter and dog, thanks in large part to our bewilderment.

I have never encountered a tribe where the badger evinced strong feelings, never met a people that loved or loathed the creature, held it sacred or told stories about it. But some years after that incident I would become acquainted with the Mongols in Khentii, who clarify badger fat into an ointment they use to treat ulcers and consumption. But neither did they view the animal as especially blessed, honourable or threatening, they regarded it rather like a herbaceous plant that could be of use.

The Siberian musk deer (*Moschus moschiferus*) is also an interesting creature, a mammal which is not a herd animal, but lives scattered over the entire Ussuri region, by all the rivers flowing westward, to be more precise. Rocky mountain crevices and crags at heights of two to three thousand feet seem to offer them ideal conditions for living. They are extremely shy and have outstanding senses. With their short legs and inconspicuous grey coat, they are kept well hidden in the mighty primeval forests in the area around the source of the Bikin, far removed from all human activity. With enormous trees lying criss-crossed, felled by old age and storms, this is virgin forest, rich in lichen and moss and it abounds with hiding places.

Once, while hunting on a ridge at dusk, I spotted a musk deer as it jumped through the fork of a three-and-a-half-metre-high oak before vanishing into dense bushes. I did not have time to fire a shot, but later managed to kill eight specimens of these ruminants, the subsequent examinations yielding very interesting results.

Not long after, I was unfortunate enough to shoot but fail to kill a hind which was facing away from me. But strangely, the injured animal did not attempt to flee, merely walked calmy in my direction, halting

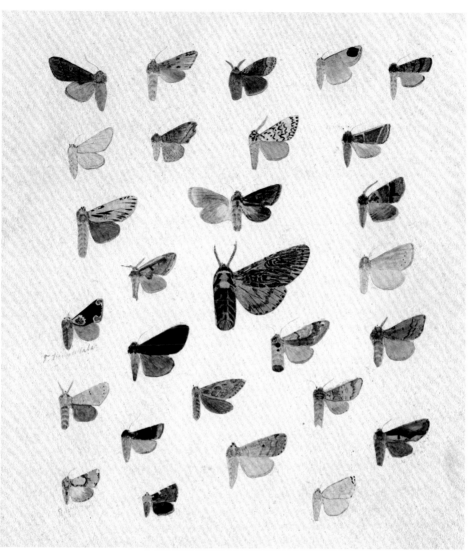

Above: These butterfly drawings are but a small fraction of those that survive. Dörries made hundreds of similar sketches during his twenty-five years in Siberia.

Left: The *Catocala doerriesi* moth, below, was named after its discoverer, Fritz Dörries, by the legendary collector Otto Staudinger.

Picus Dörriesi, Suchan, East Siberia, 1878.
Lyngipicus doerriesi, another species named
after the Dörries, most likely by an ornithologist
named Bolau.

Left: Convicts being transported. They were taken to a katorga on Sakhalin Island.

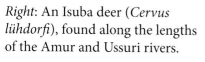

Above: Chandalaz Mountains. Here I caught 15 *Cervus dubowsky* for Hagenbeck.

Right: An Isuba deer (*Cervus lühdorfi*), found along the lengths of the Amur and Ussuri rivers.

Right: Dörries' caption indicates that this was a drawing from life, but there is no suggestion of who the man might have been.

Left: *Hyrsin Golde at the Bikin* [River], *East Siberia*. "Hyrsin" is perhaps a misspelling or Germanisation of "Hezhe". The Hezhes are one of the smallest ethnic groups in modern-day China, with a population of 4,640 in 2000.

1889. Nischnei Nowgorod Wolga.

Nizhniy Novgorod, Volga, 1889. Dörries passed through the city with his brothers Edmund and Henry on his second trip to Siberia.

A pine martin (*Martes martes*). Inspired by the local people living along the banks of the Amur River, Dörries hunted these animals using a strong steel bow.

Right: Mountain view, 2 English miles from Nagasaki, starboard side, 9th of July (left). View of an island close to Nagasaki, starboard side, 3rd of July, 6 o'clock in the morning (right).

Right: Beacon south of Sakhalin. Dörries visited Sakhalin Island but, apolitical as he was, he did not grasp the actual horrors of the prison camps there.

КАРТА

южной половины ВОСТОЧНОЙ СИБИРИ, части МОНГОЛІИ, МАНЬЧЖУРІИ и САХАЛИНА.

Масштабъ, 6750000

Къ „Общему Очерку Орографіи Восточной Сибири" П. Кропоткина. Зап. по Общ. Геогр. т. V.

Left: Dörries as a child. He was inspired to travel to Siberia at the age of four, when his father showed him an illustration of a butterfly.

Below: Dörries towards the end of his life. He set down his memoirs as a parting gift to his daughters.

three metres from me and staring with reproachful eyes, as though to remind me of the wounded deer under our linden tree in Tigrovo, not to mention the tiger who disappeared in the raging torrent. I could have fallen to my knees in shame.

I raised the rifle and shot the animal right between those eyes that spoke so directly to me, and promised myself never to shoot a female animal again, a promise I must admit I have not quite managed to keep, because as soon as summer was over I once again had to take up the rifle, and I have to confess that female animals were also shot when I was stricken with hunger. Instead, I resolved never to fire a shot at a deer unless I was certain the shot would be fatal, and *that* promise I have managed to keep.

41

In March, migratory birds arrived as usual in great multitudes, swans, geese and ducks, taking a good rest on the small tarns. As soon as the ice broke on the Bikin, the goosander (*Mergus merganser*) was in place hunting small fish, at high risk of being drawn under the ice floes.

We also caught the smaller smew (*Mergus albellus*). The flycatcher (*Muscicapa tricolor*), a beautiful little golden yellow bird, and the dark-sided flycatcher (*Muscicapa sibirica*) flew singing through the woods around the cabin, along with various species of ortolan. Sparrowhawk and besra did their best to mop up the small birds, and we acquired several specimens of them as well. And once again, several species took up residence indoors, fluttering in and out of the house as they pleased, dining with us and only too happy to sleep under our roof, particularly when it rained. At one stage we had two nuthatches and nine treecreepers (*Certhia daurica*) staying with us at the same time. And a curious observation regarding that: in nature, the treecreeper is wont to ascend tree trunks in a zigzag fashion in his search for insects in the bark. However, we, after all, were living in a log house, with similar boles, so here at first the birds moved horizontally, until they became confused or discovered their mistake, and then returned to going vertically, moving up across the logs. This was not natural to them either, but their sense of what was up and what was down seemed more fundamental than their perception of what direction a tree should point in.

Armies of different butterflies and moths turned up, each species at their own time. On the large petals of a hogweed (*Heracleum sphondylium*) I had found no fewer than eight different butterflies as well as some smaller false flower beetles, when a large Limenitis populi landed with a mighty beating of wings and chased away all the others. The beetles alone did not allow themselves to be disturbed, nor did they shrink away from the bold intruder, merely drew closer together, in the certain assurance their hard carapaces would protect them.

Out on the steppe, at a spot where we had placed a salt lick to lure deer, I discovered about forty larvae of the rare species Artona octomaculata, which I have found nowhere else in Siberia. This little black zygaenid moth, with its characteristic yellow flecks, prefers to sit on flowering geraniums. We also found a large number of golden yellow and white variants of Colias aurora, which have a predilection for the petals of the lilium (*Lilium folium*) and remained hitherto unregistered. When they finally were – several decades after our specimens found our way to Europe – they were however not attributed to us, but to another scientist.

Our collection of animals, plants, and ethnographic objects had again become so extensive that we had to ship it home. And the experience of my last trip dictated that it would be advantageous if we ourselves, with our experience in the field, assisted father with the reports and the sales.

This time I was able to convince Henry to accompany me – it was probably the thought of Mother that made the difference. On August 15, 1888, we gave our two surviving dogs to Fjodor's daughters, who had grown extremely fond of them. After our experiences with Leon and Fingauka we had resolved not to become too attached to the dogs, as all too quickly they become one's most intimate and irreplaceable friends. All the same, it was sad to part from them in this way.

We departed on two fully laden boats down the Bikin, docking at Kozslovska two days later, where I found wild apple and pear trees! A river steamer brought us up to Totalov, first on the Ussuri, then on the winding River Sungacha, and finally over Lake Khanka. Large freshwater turtles, with their smooth greyish green shells, turned out to be abundant in the Sungacha. We managed to catch three specimens by net.

On August 21, we arrived by wagon in Vladivostok. But upon finding that the next ship to Europe was not ready to sail for another six weeks, we decided to use the time collecting ethnographic items on the Korean peninsula.

We deposited our treasures with Gammenthaler – who rolled his eyes and repeated his usual mantra when we arrived thus – then we obtained the necessary merchandise to barter with, including penknives, mirrors, files, drills, buttons and colourful garments, before heading south on a hired junk, which we soon learned to manoeuvre to some degree.

After a month we had amassed more than eight hundred objects – the robes of a priestess and the uniform of a local commandant among them. We sailed back to Vladivostok, from where, five days later, a Russian steamship brought us all the way to Odessa. From there we travelled by train to Hamburg, arriving home on November 30, 1888.

42

We received, to put it mildly, a warm welcome. Mother was especially happy to have Henry home, whom she had not seen for more than ten years, when he had set out as a slight sixteen-year-old. He was now unrecognisable, a well-built man with rough features, a body full of scrapes and scars, not to mention his big Russian beard, which she, with a small, teasing smile did not grow tired of tugging at, as though to bring out the boy in him again.

To give the family an insight into what we were doing, we lined up ten or twelve bell jars in the parlour: one lays wet sand on a plate or a board, preferably of untreated wood, then stands some butterflies placed on pins down, before covering the whole thing with a bell jar. Before long, the moisture in the sand will cause the closed wings to spread. Yet another little metamorphosis, like watching a flower bloom and attain eternal life. No creature preserves itself so well in death, Mother muttered rapt, a sentence she would come to repeat, beside herself with enthusiasm over these miracles. I cannot pretend that the delicate beauty of the butterflies did not also contribute to giving her sons' lives in the field a slightly more innocent air than was actually deserved, and we were not averse to that.

*

Father assisted us as usual in describing and selling the collection. And after all the business was out of the way it only took a few days before we began to feel "farsickness", or *Fernweh*, as we called it, not least Henry, who enjoyed seeing the family and being in our childhood home, but was not comfortable in the clothes he had to wear, and was annoyed by the sounds and smells of the city, as well as eating and sleeping at fixed times, and all the routines civilisation has developed, and moreover views as progress. In the field we used watches mainly to establish the time we captured something, to measure distance, and sometimes as a compass, but rarely to govern our lives. Henry bore more than a slight resemblance to Samuel the Koryak, who could not reconcile himself to the "tropical" climate on Sidimi, something I could not resist reminding him about.

43

Our next journey would be quite different. For one thing, our youngest brother Edmund, the only one of us with a formal education in taxidermy, had returned from South America, following five years in the Amazon. And Edmund was not dissimilar to Henry and me, so he at once decided to accompany us eastward, to Mother's great sorrow.

But at least Father made no attempt to put himself forward for inclusion this time, despite our plan to travel overland to form a clearer picture of the vast Russian empire. Perhaps it was some consolation for Mother to know all three of us were together, even if it was in Siberia.

Again, we obtained the necessary assignments from Staudinger, Bolau, Noack and several others, and boarded the train in Hamburg fully equipped on April 2, 1889, with only our father on the platform this time to see us off. He had no advice or instructions, just shook us each solemnly by the hand, one after the other, and left the station before the train departed.

The journey took us via Berlin to Moscow, where I went to see the director of the Zoological Museum, an obliging old gentleman who saw the importance of our work and without too much Russian bureaucracy gave us the papers we needed. It was the official policy of the tsarist regime at this time to attract both scientific and economic interests to Siberia, the new, virgin land, the demarcation of the border with China was after all not more than twenty years old.

From Moscow we continued by train, as far east as the tracks allowed (the Trans-Siberian railway had yet to be built), and alighted in Nizhniy Novgorod, a beautiful town at the confluence of the mighty Oka and Volga rivers.

But it transpired that there was still so much ice being conveyed on the Volga that ship traffic was not under way, at least not here on the west bank. Nevertheless, we could not let that stop us, so despite deep reluctance on the part of the locals, and undoubtedly well-intentioned warnings, we purchased a barge which we loaded to the gunwales, waded out, and more or less shoved the vessel between the ice floes. We walked with water nearly up to our necks to a deafening roar.

When it grew too deep, we scrambled aboard, rowing and punting some distance, before we again had to get in and wade – most of the large rivers in Russia have shallows running lengthways, that change location from year to year, wandering ridges so to speak. When we eventually reached the east bank, we were not only soaking wet, but frozen stiff and exhausted. Fortunately, we found some accommodation nearby, and the friendly residents allowed us to dry our clothes, get warmed up and recuperate, and two days later we were on board a river steamer continuing our journey in the direction of Kazan, without encountering more ice.

44

Amongst the passengers on board we took a particular interest in the Tatars, who were both friendly and approachable. We learned about their faith, traditions and history and had ample opportunity to observe them when they performed their prayers facing the sun – how they kneeled, placed their hands on their knees, then flat on the deck, before lifting them to their foreheads, mumbling their mysterious supplications.

When, after three days, we reached Kazan, the capital of Tatarstan, we went ashore to admire the ancient city with its many churches and mosques. Women in voluminous, colourful clothes glided about like butterflies in the streets, their faces concealed behind black veils. The exoticism of the place was engrossing, making a profound impression on us, and we would have liked to stay longer, but spring was fast approaching.

We went aboard a new river steamer, sailing further along the River Kama to Perm, an industrial town founded by Peter the Great at the foot of the Urals, before travelling further by road on horse and wagon to Tyumen, on the Asian side of the mountains. In the middle of the Urals, incidentally, we passed the laconic signpost: "Europe – Asia".

*

The town of Tyumen lies on both sides of the River Tura and was at this time a large holding camp for criminals, not only Russians, but Tatars, Nogais, Bashkirs and Kyrgyz, all of whom were being sent on to eastern Siberia to build roads, or to the katorga on the island of Sakhalin.

When we arrived, large parts of the city were under water. The inhabitants were using boats between the buildings, and instead of bridges they were availing themselves of a reaction ferry consisting of six boats tied up together. The ferry itself was tethered by a rope approximately eighty feet long to the stern of another boat. This boat was anchored midstream, and the ferry was moored on the bank. When the latter was untied, the entire structure drifted right over to the opposite bank. We saw this type of ferry throughout Siberia.

In the forests around Tyumen, there lived martens and wolves as well as hares and foxes, and we were told that in winters with heavy snow, the wolves would encroach on farms and take cattle. Local hunters caught them in foothold traps. Bird migration north was under way, and flocks of ducks and geese passed above us. We even observed a sea eagle, as far from the ocean as it is possible to get on this earth.

The aforementioned detention camp was located on the bank of the Tuva, and on the day of our departure, the prisoners were being led through a funnel-like walkway down to six metal-framed cages placed one after another on large barges, which our steamboat was to tow east. They had all had half their heads shaved to render them easily recognisable. A priest was standing by the gangway to offer them some of God's words on the way, and he also handed out holy texts, which some individuals accepted with pious bows, but which most either discarded scornfully or treated in a worse manner.

We journeyed on the Tura for a few days, then on the Tobol, and on May 12 we arrived at Tobolsk, founded in the sixteenth century by the legendary Cossack Yermak, and now a picturesque town in the flattest of all lands, only horizon to see in all directions, not the slightest elevation or hill in sight, like being on the ocean.

There had once been a khanate here, but now every single inhabitant seemed to make a living from logging and lumber. On our journey further east, logs were loaded, and at one port of call we came in contact with the Ostyaks, short and stocky people who lived mainly on fish in the summertime – these truly are wetlands – but hunted different forms of wildlife in the winter. They still used bow and arrow, but – like the Golde people – also crossbow in the winter, and laid self-triggered bolts for stoats, martens and wolves. Their homes were shaped like a sugarloaf, were covered in bark and had a hole in the roof to let smoke escape. Within these gloomy, wretched conditions, they lived plagued by all sorts of vermin from childhood to old age. We bought what we could of everyday utensils and hunting implements, and were also given a glimpse into their diet, which on this particular day consisted of bread and tea, in addition to two boiled dogs' heads which they had arranged on small plates of neatly carved birch bark.

45

Each barge had room for between thirty and forty prisoners. Platforms had been built around the cages, with armed guards posted, and at every port of call we witnessed heart-rending scenes, as weeping women and children said their goodbyes to their men – for good probably, they did not seem to have many illusions about what awaited them in the katorga. Some of the prisoners looked devastated, others were defiant and aggressive. We saw one who pulled at and pounded on the iron bars, looking like he wanted to attack both his wife and children, who were left behind crying on the riverbank, after bidding him a final farewell on his Via Dolorosa.

On one of the barges, separated from the men, were three women with children who had been granted permission to travel with their husbands. We learned that the government would provide for them when they finally arrived, in exchange for their settling in the east when their husbands' sentences were served and agreeing never to return to Russia.

Hard labour was determined by what sort of crime one had committed. Those guilty of the most grievous offences were sent without mercy to the mines, while others had to build roads in the Amur and Ussuri regions, construct bridges, and eventually the railway. Their upkeep, by and large, seemed passable, as far as we could see. Furthermore, several of the political prisoners were quite prosperous and could make the trip easier by means of bribes.

The entire leg of the journey from Tyumen to Tomsk – with the final stretch on the River Ob – was uneventful. At one stop I went ashore and while there noticed six prisoners standing together in their cage talking in low voices. Another prisoner joined them, the only one whose face was properly shaved. As there were no razors or knives of any kind on board, I grew curious and called out to them. The freshly shaved prisoner held up a knife with a triumphant smile, it turned out to be a shard of a cup that he had honed to sharpness against the bars.

We arrived in Tomsk, a small town back then, on May 20. And as soon as we moored up, two prisoners managed to escape, causing a furore amongst the guards and equal rejoicing amongst their fellows. There were signs of a revolt, but it was soon suppressed. And the worst convicts were placed in leg irons when the next stage of the journey by land was set to commence. This would take them via Krasnoyarsk and Irkutsk, a distance of more than 1,750 kilometres, each day's march covering between twenty and thirty kilometres. Any of them who collapsed along the way were allowed sit or lie down in a wagon, together with the women and children.

We were told there were shacks set up at certain points along the road where the prisoners could spend the night. From Irkutsk, the procession would then travel on to Lake Baikal, where they would be transported by boat across to the Asian side. Then they had to travel by foot, over Nizhne Udinsk to Shilka, in other words another 1,030 kilometres, until they reached the banks of the Amur, where yet another river steamer would take them aboard in new cages and tow them on barges down to the Sea of Okhotsk and over to their final destination, the katorga on the island of Sakhalin.

46

We parted ways with the pitiful transport in Tomsk and within fifteen days had made it to Irkutsk ourselves by horse and wagon.

Irkutsk is situated on the River Angara and was, from the 1820s onwards, developed by the so-called Decembrists, political prisoners who were exiled here following a failed revolt against the tsar. They were much wealthier and more privileged than the prisoners we had travelled with, and the city, without doubt the most beautiful in Siberia, bore signs of that. I would draw particular attention to the huge bazaar halls, the nomads' junctions between China, Mongolia and Russia.

After resupplying and taking a few days to look around, we travelled on by wagon to the small village of Listvyanka on the western shores of Lake Baikal, where a division of Cossacks loaned us a dilapidated stable.

Baikal is the largest and deepest lake on earth. Geophysicist V.B. Shostakovich has calculated that it holds 23,000 cubic versts of water; lying there at the foot of those ever-white Asian mountain ranges, it is bluer than the Mediterranean and so boundlessly beautiful that once a person has set eyes upon it, they will always carry the sight with them.

Initially we only intended to survey birdlife and vegetation on the

Asian side, even though the migration was virtually over. Some fishermen rented us a sailboat, albeit reluctantly, thinking no doubt that three German gentlemen city-dwellers would not be able to manoeuvre it, but fortunately we were able to compensate them handsomely.

We crossed the enormous lake, soon discovering that conditions could shift as quickly as on the ocean, it was like the Bay of Biscay. We were forced to seek safe haven and remain moored up for a day and a night. But then the summer storm passed as quickly as it had come upon us. We followed the eastern shore northwards, a peaceful sail past broad valleys, narrow ravines and precipitous mountainsides, an extravagant feast for the eyes. Darkness was falling as we landed south of the mouth of the River Bargusin. Above us, the mountainsides were ablaze in full bloom, mostly Spirea chamaedryfolia and Spirea flexuosa, but also daylily (*Hemerocallis*) and the larger-flowered trollius, with stamens preferred by small bugs.

In daylight the next morning we could really take in the riches of our surroundings: the innumerable root leaves of the buttercup family (*Ranunculaceae*), especially larkspur and globeflower (*Trollius*), adorning the many tree trunks that had fallen to the ground, so buried under lichen and moss that they formed their own landscapes.

We stumbled on, negotiating obstacles, and found our way through man-high aconites. The riverbanks were covered with ribes bushes with roots stretching over the stream, sending up new shoots on the other sides. Rockfoil (*Saxifraga aestivalis*) grew abundantly beneath the protection of the foliage. Saxifraga crassifolia grew half out in the water, the leaves of which the inhabitants of the area used to make tea. There was also marsh marigold (*Caltha*) to be found, and around the small brooks, the cloudberries (*Rubus chamaemorus*) and stone brambles (*Rubus saxatilis*) created an illuminated floor suspended above the spongy surface.

In the ravines we found the red-flowered Turk's cap lily (*Lilium martagon*) that along with geraniums forms a rainbow of colour. Tall valerians grew side by side with light blue columbines (*Aquilegia*). In the corries, spruce and pine grew so densely that no sunbeam could penetrate. The birdsong was overwhelming. On a huge fallen and moss-covered tree, we saw a marten (*Martes sibirica*) pursue a squirrel, without any luck, its quarry got to safety at the top of a pine tree. In the birch thicket, the arctic redpoll sang, and by the streams the thrush stood perfectly still in anticipation of small worms and other delicacies.

I also encountered a deer – a wapiti – that supposedly lived much further north, on what the Russians call the Vitim Plateau, and that type of deer would later lead me on one of my most gruelling escapades, possibly as a direct result of the report I would write on this very expedition.

Neither were wolves and foxes a rarity. Everything was duly noted and described; we kept a record on landscape, vegetation, animals and meteorological conditions, and Edmund prepared like there was no tomorrow, he was in his element here. When challenged to choose between the Amazon and Siberia, he replied "both" and of that he had absolutely no doubt.

47

After just a few days we had to leave the fantastic nature behind and take ourselves back to Listvyanka, where we prepared the rest of the haul and rested for a time.

It was still too early in the year for butterflies, but in the valleys to the south and east of Lake Baikal we recorded several species of Argynnis and Lycaenae, resting with wings raised close to brooks on the mountain slopes. Here, like everywhere in the area, flew the painted lady (*Vanessa cardui*), including some of last year's specimens. We did not see any golden eagles, though we were informed that they inhabited the area. We did, on the other hand, again observe sea eagles, and on numerous occasions, no small miracle this far inland. And we could admire the brazen black kite at any time, hearing its singsong whistling as, along with the ravens, it followed the fishing boats out to sea; they were legion in the afternoon as they sat waiting for entrails and waste just a few metres from the fishermen and their wretched cabins.

The collector loves the sounds of nature, but in fact, it was rather quiet by Baikal. In the evenings we could, of course, hear the rush of streams, but the rivers in the region are silent and slow-flowing, and the quivering reflection of the moonlight on the lake created a peculiar silence, as though the land were holding its breath.

And where was the nightingale?

Siberia has a species with a much finer plumage than Europe's indefatigable artist, and its song is most certainly the equal of ours. The rubythroat emits its beautiful tones both day and night. And the delicate sound of its beak against the bark of trees only accentuated the silence.

48

We had as usual been asked by the Museum of Ethnology to examine the tribes in the region. And it is in the main Buryats and the Tungusic people who live by Lake Baikal, the former along the south-western shore and upon the island of Olkhon, the largest on Lake Baikal, covering all of 730 square kilometres, where they subsist mainly on sheep farming and fishing. The Buryats also hunt nerpa (*Phoca sibirica*), a rotund fresh-water species of seal only found here.

The Tungusic people, on the other hand, live at the north-eastern end of the lake, and further north towards Jakutia. The two groups are very different, with regard to both physique and facial features, and above all, temperament and character.

The Tungusic people we met were cheerful, attentive, open and bold, whilst the Buryats seemed indifferent, almost sad, and I would not hesitate to call them phlegmatic. They are nomads and fishermen and live in smoke-filled, dirty yurts. As many of their number are islanders, living in such an isolated spot, the Russians have yet to have the same influence on their way of life as they have had on the Transbaikalan Buryats living to the east and south of the lake.

The Buryats belong to the larger Chorin tribe. They live in extended family groups, build villages, and are passionate adherents of tobacco and spirits. They purchase their tobacco from the Russians but smoke it in Chinese paper, often already from the age of eight.

When the harvest is celebrated, they sit cross-legged around a fire waiting for sour mare's milk to be thrice distilled as specified, certain individuals already three sheets to the wind. And consequently, a Buryat's temperament will alter completely. From being mild and well-mannered, he turns quarrelsome. Respect for age, laws, gender and friendship gives way to violent altercations; most crimes are committed while in an inebriated state.

There is nothing to be gained by socialising with the otherwise so amiable members of the tribe on such days – we later experienced similar behaviour among the Mongols. But when the rage is finally supplanted by weary exhaustion, the old peace soon re-emerges in these sober souls, and even the most serious offence is forgotten, disappearing as quickly as a child's patience.

Like the Tungusic people, the Buryats enjoy a seal speciality which they eat raw, holding the blubber in their mouths, rending it with their teeth and sucking it in as wet slime, and it does not taste good, that I can attest to. I also observed the Buryats in the Yablonovy Mountains partake of seal in this way.

A drink called *Ziepeltee* had obviously particular status and was only for the wealthy. It was prepared with salt and fat, sometimes milk, and my brothers and I could not agree whether it tasted divine or diabolical. Edmund was full of praise for it and bought three large pitchers. The Buryats bartered to get corn from the Russians, but have no grinders, so they ground it by stamping on it with wooden shoes.

Some of the Tungusic people kept reindeer, and large herds were an unmistakable symbol of wealth and status. They also mainly sewed clothes from reindeer hide, but also from red deer. Their homes, which they called *haran*, were constructed around a conical frame of fifteen to twenty poles covered with bark, mostly of birch. When they roam, they leave the construction standing and build a new one when necessary. A wandering Tungus always carries seven items, comprising really all his property:

1. A bear spear, 2¾ metres long, whittled from birch, carved knots a foot's distance along it, with a sharp iron tip (1½ toll wide, 9 toll long and ½ toll thick). Two barbs are fitted below the head, to prevent the spear penetrating the bear too deeply; if it becomes lodged without the thrust being fatal, the hunter is finished.
2. A gun, both stock and barrel always sheathed in reindeer hide, which is only removed prior to firing.
3. A pigtail, for driving away flies and mosquitoes.
4. A Chinese pipe, usually brass.
5. A boat, with the frame and deck constructed from birch-bark, a light, useful vessel in wetlands and small lakes.
6. The harpoon they hunt fish with.
7. Suede clothing, fur in winter.

We acquired examples of all these items, except for the boat, of which we made several sketches, making it possible to reconstruct in museums back home.

Within both tribes (and I believe this pertains to all Siberian peoples), the woman has lower status than the man. While he is free to indulge his desires, the woman is subordinate to him. She gives birth, looks after and raises the children, makes food, tans leather, herds reindeer and helps on the hunt. Without her the man would be lost.

49

We left Listvyanka by horse and wagon, crossing the Baikal Mountains to the south. After barely a week we had reached the old Russian fort at Troitskosavsk (Kyakhta), now only a village, its main income being the tea caravans passing on their way from Peking to Irkutsk, two-wheeled horse-carts for the most part, with four bales of tea on each, sewn inside pigskins.

We followed the Mongolian border east towards Khentii, and after some minor hardships – helping the horses tug the wagon through the deep desert sand amongst others – we arrived at the Khentii Mountains, the first goal on our journey, a little-explored region, and the very reason that Staudinger had sent us.

Within a week, we had constructed a spacious log dwelling by a small mountain stream, which would serve as both abode and workplace for the remainder of the summer. And at about the same time the insects came to life.

The Khentii Mountains extend south from Russia into Mongolia and are, in my opinion, part of the same geological formation as the Yablonovy range, the apple mountains. And we soon developed a particular predilection for the Colias genus, or clouded yellows, a migratory butterfly that would not survive winters here but rather travels hundreds of miles up from the south every summer. It lays its eggs, which become larvae, then pupae, and finally butterflies, then migrates several hundred miles south again, a butterfly of passage.

The clouded yellow, in common with other butterflies, has no lungs but rather tiny perforations in the exoskeleton (of chitin) that oxygen passes through on its way to the vital organs. Using its elongated mouthpart (proboscis), the butterfly sucks nectar from the deepest flowers, then lays its orange eggs, preferably on the leaves of a lucerne (*Medicago sativa*).

We also discovered a new species of Colias, which Staudinger later chose to name after Tamerlane (*Colias tamerlana*), also known as Timur Lenk (Timur the lame), the Mongolian leader who swept across the steppes like the wind with his brutal armies, killing and conquering as he went in the fourteenth century.

At night, we stretched a linen sheet at an angle from the forest floor up to a stand about a metre high, before illuminating the sheet with small flashes from a lantern, thus collecting an incredible number of midges, flies and moths in just a few hours. At its most intense, Edmund was hard put to keep up with us.

Our little brother also began working on a theory that butterflies must have sense organs in their legs to be able to recognise the host plants for their eggs – how else was a Colias able to pick out a lucerne in a sea of enticing alternatives? We first viewed the theory as a bold one but leaned further and further in the same direction the more observations we made, and the hypothesis would be confirmed many years later, although unfortunately not attributed to Edmund.

50

Khentii was also home to predators. It should be noted that the wolves we had become accustomed to in eastern Siberia were of a calmer disposition than those we encountered here in Central Asia. We could observe packs of wolves hunting livestock and domestic animals within settlements, even in broad daylight in the middle of summer, when there is usually an abundance of all kinds of prey in the wild.

Late one evening, I had just shot a fine-looking roebuck with particularly interesting antlers (which now adorn the wall of my study!) and was making my way back to the cabin with the animal over my shoulders. It was night, but in the flickering light of a dying campfire outside I could make out a large stone I had not noticed previously.

I gave it a kick and was struck by how strangely soft it was. The next moment it disappeared. I dropped the buck and held my rifle at the ready. By the campfire lay an old Russian hunter we had let spend the night, along with his three dogs, all sleeping peacefully. Henry and Edmund were inside the cabin, also asleep.

A short time later, I was standing in the doorway eating some black bread, when one of the hunter's dogs came over to keep me company. As I was tossing him a few scraps of bread a wolf suddenly brushed past my left leg and tried to get the better of the dog. It failed, however, and vanished as quickly as it had appeared.

I went inside to go to bed, exhausted as I was, but awoke after a while to aggressive barking. I jumped up, ran outside and in the semi-darkness saw a big, bewildering skein of wolves and dogs in a life-or-death struggle. And again, the wolves lost out and left. But the strange thing was that the Russian hunter slept soundly throughout, and neither Henry nor Edmund so much as opened an eyelid.

Later, it turned out that what I had believed to be a stone was in fact one of a pair of criminals who most likely had plans to attack us, my arrival home no doubt thwarting them in that endeavour. We learned they had stabbed some people to death in a nearby village. Fortunately, some peasants managed to capture them and clap them in irons.

In mid-July, Henry and I departed for a fifteen-day butterfly hunt higher up in the Yablonovy Mountains, whilst Edmund rode off to the afore-mentioned village, as criminals still abounded in the area.

Up in the mountains, we found accommodation on a holding rented by a freed convict, a Nogai of Turkish origin, whom we immediately hit it off with. We were now working at an altitude of 5,500 feet, so frost on the higher slopes in the mornings was not uncommon. Amongst other beautiful species, we got hold of the nimble Colias viluiensis, and at night the much sought-after noctuid, or owlet moth, Plusiinae dives, as it sat shivering and half frozen on an artemisia flower, it is also a migrant, covering vast distances each year.

In Yablonovy, the two red flowering lily species of Lilium martagon and Lilium tenuifolias are particularly abundant, well anchored in the stony ground so they avoid being torn up by the perpetual wind. We found Rheum compactum everywhere. Even at a height of 4,500 feet this rhubarb plant was common.

51

While collecting butterflies I have eyes for little else, so I was startled when, in a dense thicket, I suddenly came face to face with another person, a primitive person at that, clothed in a worn-out hessian sack, with carelessly cut-out holes for the arms and neck, his head wreathed in shoulder-length dark hair and an unkempt beard that waved in the breeze, a giant of a man, with an ashen face filled with resignation.

When I asked him what he was doing out here in the wilderness, he wordlessly offered me a piece of bread. I had not seen bread in days so gladly accepted and handed him what food I had, some smoked meat. We sat eating and he told me that in his younger years he had been a soldier in Moscow, but had served under a company commander who meted out punishment on a whim, a pure sadist, until one day the soldiers had had enough and drew lots on who among them would put a stop to his odious practices.

"I drew the longest straw," he said, in a croaky voice.

One morning, while they were engaged in target practice, he had shot the captain off his horse. But unfortunately, it was only a flesh wound. The officer recovered and the guilty party was condemned to hard labour for life in a coal mine on Sakhalin.

After eight years in the katorga he had managed to escape and, for a time, hid amongst the Ainu on the north of the island. But somebody must have betrayed him, because he was recaptured, punished with fifty lashes and forced to spend many more years in the pits, both day and night, with shackles on his ankles.

Eventually, together with six fellow prisoners, he conceived yet another plan to escape. One stormy night they made their way, avoiding detection, down to a cove where they had seen a Japanese fishing boat seek shelter. When the storm lifted, they forced the fishermen to bring them to the mainland.

But there was, as he put it, nothing over there, and the already exhausted men faced a difficult future. They were close to starving to death when by blind chance they stumbled into a Gilyak settlement by the mouth of the Amur.

The natives gave them food and clothing, as well as bows, arrows and a crossbow. For a while they wandered in the forests after wild animals and birds. But none of them were hunters, so mostly they stole salmon from the natives' nets and lived on plants and berries from the forest. To cut a long story short:

"Over the course of the following two years, I lost all six of my comrades, one by one they either succumbed to the cold or starved to death."

Nevertheless, one thing was clear to him: he was never going back to Sakhalin! If a fugitive is caught a second time, they are given one hundred and fifty lashes, and no-one survives that, because the guards use the most brutish prisoner to mete out this punishment

He looked straight at me:

"It might be cold comfort, but one day fate will catch up with him too, when he has served his time and goes to live as a settler someplace here in the east – then sooner or later an escaped prisoner will show up and hack him to death with an axe, believe you me."

Overcoming many difficulties, he had followed the Amur upriver and was now heading to Mongolia, where he hoped to be of some use to either the Buryats or the Mongols, as a shepherd for instance. But he was without papers and had hoped we might be of some help, which was why he had made his presence known, he said, we seemed trustworthy – did I know of anybody he could turn to?

I congratulated him drily on our failure to notice we were being watched, thanked him for the trust he placed in me and said I could speak with the commander in Khentii, but that it was several days' walk, and truth be told I had little hope the Cossacks would help a fugitive.

He nodded heavily.

We finished our meal, and I took him to the Nogai's farm. He was given food, clothing and a bed and stayed on for a time. He tended to the animals, helped with the haying, and was a quiet, humble, industrious worker. We all grew very fond of him, especially the children on the farm. But in the long run nothing could keep him, and one morning he said his goodbyes and continued on towards Mongolia, and I have not heard from him since. He never told us his name, and it seems to me that was only fitting.

52

We were working, as I have already mentioned, at altitudes of four to five thousand feet, and up so high there were only plants with minimal leaf forms. However, even higher up, I found the rare Parnassius tenedius butterfly. Somewhat lower down floated the large Parnassius apollo sibiricus, which we described as a new species. And a little further down again in the valleys, we also came across the beautiful Parnassius nomion, our old friend from the drawing from childhood. On an island in the River Chikoy in the south of the Yablonovy range, we recorded, to our great surprise, wild currants (*Ribes fragrans*) in full bloom. There were also wild gooseberries, with their delicious red, ovoid fruits, to be found in all the valleys.

In addition, we observed many Melitaea and Argynnis, and amongst them the very rare A. amphilochus and A. eugenia, much sought after amongst European collectors. And let me not forget the exotic Colias melinos, Colias aurora, and once again the even rarer Colias viluiensis, which Staudinger would express great pride in being able to incorporate into his collection.

*

We were happy in Khentii: every day offered something fresh and unforeseen, new species and new landscapes, we had the food and water we needed and wanted for nothing.

But we noticed that the Mongols, unlike the Tungus people and the Buryats, did not eat fish and would in fact rather go hungry. When we enquired as to why they did not partake of this abundance found in even the smallest stream and that we ate all the time, we were told that fish were viewed as a snake or serpent. And the serpent was not so far removed from the dragon, the most accursed creature of all.

But perhaps an old legend the children in the region learn is equally pertinent in this regard. It concerns the world's largest salmon, a taimen (*Hucho taimen*), which some hungry Mongols in a mythical time found frozen in the river ice. They hacked through the ice, cut a few pieces off, and thus survived the winter. But when spring came, the fish thawed, grew stronger, visited the Mongol's village and ate all the inhabitants.

I do not know if it was our consumption of fish that was to blame, or some other foreign feature, but one day the locals decided they did not want us there any longer. We were told that a so-called oracle, an old woman, had prophesied:

"When the Germans catch our butterflies, the sun will no longer shine and the grain will not ripen."

We were therefore encouraged to leave, something we of course could not agree to. Leave this paradise? We continued about our business undeterred. And one night, five armed civilians emerged from the forest and lined up with weapons at the ready just thirty metres from the house and called for us to come out and confess our misdeeds.

We were busy indoors and shouted back that that was out of the question, making it clear we would return fire if they attempted violence of any type, showing our gun barrels in the doorway for good measure. They stood conferring with each other for a while, but fortunately finally saw sense and departed sulkily. They were most likely neither soldiers nor hunters. And following this incident we did not encounter any more problems with the local inhabitants.

53

I must make mention of the fate of yet another person that made an impression on me in the mountains. I was roaming alone with the net one day when I happened upon a cabin I had not noticed before, even though I had passed that way several times, as it was hidden in a narrow hollow and well camouflaged.

I knocked on the door and on receiving no answer, opened it and went in. Inside, there was a low-set bed with a surface of dried grass and a worn blanket. The rest of the room was bare apart from a home-made table and a chopping block. On the wall hung a birch-bark bag containing a tattered children's primer in Russian, with pictures of animals. That was it. And the owner was unfortunately not at home.

But I wanted to make his acquaintance, and on my return the following day, I saw the door was open. I called out, asking if anyone was there. Just then a medium-sized brown bear emerged from the bushes and sat down like a dog awaiting scraps at the entrance. I saw it pick up something and realised it was being fed. After five minutes the door closed, and papa bear ambled off. I walked a little closer and called out "Good morning" in Russian:

"*Dobroe utro.*"

The door reopened and the tall, barefooted figure of a man in a long, grey smock appeared in the doorway. He resembled a suntanned monk, his features sombre and grim. He had long silver hair and a thin white beard that reached halfway down his chest.

He caught sight of me and signalled for me to enter with a wave of his hand. I accepted the invitation and, finding him seated on the bed when I entered, sat down on the chopping block. He looked at me earnestly and asked:

"What are you doing here?"

I replied that I just had to make the acquaintance of the owner of this cabin, who I had understood was an animal lover, as I was myself, and it was my reason for visiting the area, in addition to being a man of science.

He offered me a gnarled hand and said:

"We're sure to get along."

But then he fell silent and just sat looking down at his knuckles. I remembered the old primer in the birch bag and pictured how often he must have thumbed through it. Some minutes passed and I could not help but think of the last hermit I had encountered, that these men were not used to talking, that it had been an eternity since they had seen another person, much like myself when I journeyed through Japan.

Then he cleared his throat and proceeded unsolicited – albeit haltingly and slowly – to tell me that while in the vigour of youth he had been condemned to death for sedition and had one spring day stood together with three hundred others in a prison yard in Moscow awaiting execution. Whilst the prisoners stood talking amongst themselves about the bleak future facing Russia, another three names were called and herded towards the place of execution. The next moment, however, a messenger arrived with new orders from the tsar: the executions were to cease, and the remaining prisoners were to serve life sentences building roads in the Amur region. Everybody breathed a sigh of relief. Because, as he said: "We had no idea that henceforth we were assigned a fate worse than death."

His decrepit body shook with sobs. He tried to collect himself and, fumbling, produced a birch-bark bowl filled with blueberries, each the size of a small plum, and very bitter, I only ate them myself when there was no water nearby. But since I had bread to share with him, and it would even out the taste, I accepted his offer.

After sixteen years he had managed to escape.

"We couldn't take any more."

Thirty-two prisoners had broken out of the camp and joined in a conspiracy of sorts, wandering over the next few years raiding village after village, robbing, burning and killing. And he had been swept along in this, whether he wanted it or not. But on one occasion he was in a dwelling and a pretty young girl had put up resistance.

"I can still picture her dark eyes. I yelled, 'Get out, all we want is food!' But she wouldn't obey, and I plunged my knife into her chest, and she collapsed. I can't have been in my right mind. One last look from those dying eyes told me I was no longer a human. And shortly afterwards I parted ways with the gang.

"Now I have lived here alone in Khentii for almost ten years. Now and again a passing hunter will give me some bread and tea, otherwise I live for the animals, only by giving to them can I make up for my trespasses against mankind."

Then he stood abruptly and solemnly declared:

"When a bear one day breaks my bones, I will breathe my last as an animal, without the least complaint."

54

During the summer we had, in addition to butterflies and birds, collected a considerable quantity of antlers, primarily in the areas south of Lake Baikal and in Transbaikal, but also in Korotkovo, Minuslansk, and Achinask in Yablonovy. In Khentii we acquired some magnificent and some very abnormal specimens. We were unable, however, to chart the migration of the deer. The six- to eight-year-old bucks we killed for our own domestic use all weighed between eighty and eighty-five pounds, that is approximately twice as much as our German bucks. With regard to the rutting times of the animals, I have noted: by the east Siberian coast on September 11, at Ussuri on August 21, and in Transbaikal on July 27.

It was time for us to leave Khentii, as snow could fall in the mountains any day, so we packed our treasures and equipment onto the wagon, took our leave of the log cabin and made our way to the bank of the River Chikoy, where we came upon a small Buryat village not indicated on Kropotkin's map. I marked it, giving it the name Igorski, since the only Russian we encountered there introduced himself as Igor.

He was of very diminutive stature, almost a dwarf, bald, about fifty years of age, with strangely white skin and he dressed like the natives. He was pleasant and approachable and seemed to speak most languages. But we did not find out where he was from nor what he was doing there.

In any case, he helped us bargain with the Buryats, who did not speak Russian. We needed two boats and were willing to offer the horses and wagon in return, but initially they were extremely reluctant, claiming that there in the upper reaches of the Chikoy, the river was barely navigable, but these warnings were accompanied by peculiar laughter.

According to the map, the drop in the river towards the north-east was stupendous, close to a thousand metres, but this was spread over almost three hundred versts. Whatever the dangers, Igor was energetic in his haggling, if that was indeed what he was doing, because it was not cheap, even with the horse and wagon as a makeweight. But the boats appeared to be both new and robust.

We loaded our chests aboard, tethered and covered them with water-repellent canvas, then bade goodbye to the village and little Igor, who stood on the bank waving a flag. Edmund and I sat in the second boat and joked that if we sank now, then our last sight before we were consigned to the everlasting would be the image of a white, Russian dwarf on a riverbank in the wilderness waving a Mongolian flag.

And I have to admit, it was a hazardous voyage, we were already moving at breakneck speed only two or three versts after we cast off. It further degenerated into pure madness. We hurtled through one raging rapid after another, and Henry's boat – which we had agreed on keeping fifteen to twenty metres ahead – could barely be discerned amid the roaring waters. There were enormous tree trunks floating in all directions, lumber that had been taken in earlier ice drifts and high water.

The boats constantly hit trees and stones, and how Henry managed on his own ahead is a mystery to me. I was happy that I had Edmund in the bow, who had navigated rapids in South America and thus had some experience. He even went as far as to allow himself a triumphant smile every time we avoided capsizing by the skin of our teeth.

One rainbow after another curved through the gorges. We had little concept of which way was up or down, and on the rare occasions the river god paused for breath, we bailed water for dear life. Henry managed to tie the oar to the stern, using it as a tiller of sorts, and bailed water as best he could as well. If I had had the faintest inkling of how it would be, we would never have set off. Now I recalled the Buryats' strange smiles, and Igor with the flag. At least my brothers had something to tease me about for the rest of my life: "Do you remember those altitude measurements of yours, Fritz, in Chikoy?"

We slept at night in a tent on the bank. We were cold and wet and had great difficulty lighting fires, but fortunately were so exhausted that we slept a few hours anyway. After three days, the river became deeper and calmer, the terrain was still precipitous and dramatic, but the rapids were fewer, and we could go further in from the sodden bank when we stopped to sleep for the night.

By noon on the fifth day, we were through the worst of it, and went ashore to patch up the boats and investigate a sheer rockface about one hundred and fifty feet in height, east of the river. It turned out the entire massif consisted of pure anthracite. What hidden riches this land holds!

Furthermore, we were surprised by several Siberian jays (*Perisoreus infaustus*), birds considered a bad omen. So we shot five of them, with some sense of triumph after surviving the upper reaches of the river, and after taking some interesting damselflies, we continued on.

Over the following days, the river calmed further, growing steadily wider, the landscape levelling out gently, and the journey began to border on the pleasant. Moreover, we were now dry and warm and could enjoy the stunning scenery in comfort.

One day, we spotted a grotto in a rockface and paddled to shore. Whilst Henry and Edmund prepared food, I clambered up to the opening and into the grotto, which grew narrower and narrower the higher I went. Cold air flowed down upon me like ice-cold water. When I could get no higher, I was able to just about discern an opening twenty or thirty metres above me, with clear, blue sky showing. I began to search around in the dim light and came upon the remains of a mammoth, frozen in ice about five metres thick. Heavy rain and cascading water had formed this grotto and exposed parts of the prehistoric animal. As proof, I took two molars that were lying beside the carcass; one weighed just over two kilos, the other around three.

55

In the little village of Krasny Chikoy there lived a group of Old Believers, so-called *Semeyskie*, from the old Russian word for "family", a people who in the eighteenth century had refused to submit to Patriarch Nikon's reformation of the church, had been banished to the east and now lived in small, remote enclaves over large parts of Siberia. And no group preserved Russian traditions better than the Old Believers, with regard to building methods, furnishings, clothes, customs, and of course the liturgies and everything surrounding matters of faith. We also had the opportunity to hear their indescribably beautiful, polyphonic singing during a mass, albeit from a spot outside the church we were directed to in an authoritative manner, "infidels" that we were.

Fortunately, we were able to sell the battered boats. And for the price we ourselves had paid for them, plus four wolf skins and a bear hide, the Russians let us take possession of a decent wagon. We had no problems renting horses, as the village was located along a postal route. We then set off overland, east towards Chita, a distance close to six hundred versts.

We arrived one night at a way station during a heavy storm and went in to get something to eat. I asked the station keeper to hitch up new horses, since we did not plan on staying the night. He tried to talk us out of it, both on account of the weather and because the road ahead went through a forest. I demurred, saying neither forests nor thunderstorms frightened us, and we usually travelled by night to save time. He then told me that the area was crawling with criminals.

"I lost one of my coachmen just over a week ago. Both he and his passenger were shot, most likely in an ambush, and everything of value was taken, the horse returned alone with the wagon a few days later."

"Unfortunately, we have no gendarmerie here," he added, "who could pursue and shoot the scum."

Two Mongolian monks who were intending to stay the night heard what we were talking about and came and sat at our table. One of them told us how they had been robbed of a money pouch containing two thousand roubles, as well as many important papers the previous night.

"But you're both still alive, gentlemen, how can that be?"

The thieves had sneaked up silently from behind, hung onto the back of the wagon, and simply cut through the canopy and snatched the pouch, which lay beneath a pillow. The monks had realised something was afoot:

"I fired two shots, but I don't think I hit anything."

I turned to the station keeper:

"Well, that's two warnings we've been given, you've both done your duty, but I'd still like you to hitch up three good horses, of course we'll be responsible should anything befall them, so send a coachman along also."

It had stopped raining by the time we went back outside, with only the occasional flash of lightning here and there in the black sky. And with loaded rifles resting across our knees, we continued on our way at a fast pace. Nothing happened in the first hour, nor in the second, but all the same I had a feeling that all was not as it should be. We moved from where we were sitting in the back of the wagon, took up prone firing positions beside the coachman and asked him to go even faster.

Just before a swing in the road, the horses made a startled sideways jump. We realised something on the road must have spooked them. Shortly afterwards we heard two shots, followed by two more, but none of us were hit. We returned fire, out into the air, mostly as a warning, because we had seen no muzzle flash. Lying in the same positions, we continued through the forest unhindered, arriving at the next station at dawn. That was when we noticed two bullet holes in the leather canopy above our heads. We settled with the coachman, rented new horses and proceeded on our journey.

As if the events of that night were not enough, on the next stretch of our journey we were witness to the conclusion of a similar drama. At the time, the post was not transported by train as it is today, but by horse and wagon in summer and by sleigh in winter. Once or twice a week, these equipages travelled throughout Siberia, from station to station, changing horse teams, and earlier that summer a large sum of money had been sent from Sretensk to Irkutsk.

A station keeper and one of his coachmen got wind of this, and together with a Jew from Chita, had laid plans to rob this transport. When the equipage passed a prearranged spot in the woods, the station keeper and the Jew were lying in wait. The soldier on duty, sitting with a loaded gun atop the mailbags, was simply shot, and the horses and wagon led into the woods, the money stolen, and the mailbags buried with the dead soldier.

Sometime later, the coachman, who felt he had been cheated out of his fair share of the haul, let his tongue run away with him while he was out carousing one night. The disappearance and robbery were solved, the murder discovered, and the buried remains of the soldier and the mailbags found.

It was the conclusion to this drama we were now witness to on the outskirts of Nerchinsk.

The three murderers were led out from a makeshift gaol, each wrapped in white canvas sacks, tied at their ankles, and nooses were placed around their necks. Between fifty and sixty onlookers had gathered around the place of execution, and the Cossack in charge was about to release the trapdoor when a macabre scene unfolded: the leader of the band, the station keeper, was a very fat man, and as he lurched and struggled the trapdoor opened, but the rope snapped, and he landed on the ground with a thud. He soon raised himself upright and, performing the oddest hops and twists, began to curse and abuse both the spectators and the Russian authorities, even the tsar was told off in no uncertain terms. They had to hang him anew, and on this second attempt succeeded.

The Jew sobbed and begged for his life, he had a large family and was innocent, he claimed, but he was not believed and was also hanged. As was the coachman.

56

From Nerchinsk, we went further east through the gentlest landscape Siberia has to offer, rolling green hills with lush meadows and forests, like an eastern Tyrol, and arrived in the village of Sretensk on the banks of the River Shilka. Here we sold the wagon, loaded the collections and equipment aboard a river steamer and travelled down the Shilka to where it meets the Argun, forming the mighty Amur, the largest and longest of the boundary rivers between Russia and China.

From the confluence, we sailed on downriver to the town of Blagoveshchensk, arriving on September 5, having covered close to two thousand miles since we left our flag-waving friend Igor in Khentii, by water, land and water again.

In Blagoveshchensk we disembarked from the steamer and bought a roomy boat for sixty roubles. We sailed this further downriver on the Amur, towards the town of Radeffka, or Radde, as the capital of the Jewish Autonomous Oblast is called today. And this eleven-day voyage on the astounding Amur was to be one of my life's greatest experiences. Amur means "big river" in Evenk, or "great water", whilst the Chinese call it *Heilongjiang*, "Black Dragon River", and with good reason.

*

At night, we slept on board the boat, which had a little roof at the stern, and let the current carry us leisurely through the magical darkness. Starry skies, cosmic tranquillity and a lasting languor, and a faint rustle now and again from the reeds along the banks. The Amur is a sea in motion, through the most formidable landscape. We listened to the second movement of Beethoven's Seventh, which we had grown up with, and Edmund, who is not the most talkative, began telling us about the Amazon, and how he had never expected to experience anything similar in the northern hemisphere – here the orchestra of the rain forest was replaced by the silence of the taiga. He spoke of the mosquitoes, the heat, and of the true nature of all rivers, how they divide the land for evermore, supplying both sides with the exact same amount of life-giving power. I would look back on this leg of the journey with longing in years to come, when I found myself again in the same area, only in appalling conditions.

While en route we fished extensively. We ate salmon, pike (*esox lucius*) and burbot (*Lota lota*) in the main, but also catfish (*Silurus glanis*). As the Russians say: "The pike is in the water so that the carp is not lost in reverie." And we learned from the locals how to catch taimen using live mice as bait. The taimen is, as I have mentioned, the world's largest salmon and lives in most of the big rivers in Siberia. They can reach weights of fifty kilos, and we caught several close to thirty. It tastes delicious, whether fried, boiled or smoked.

We also tried to catch ourselves a kaluga (*Huso dauricus*), the largest type of sturgeon living here in the east, an anadromous species, which migrates out to sea, simply because as a new-born larva it is carried downstream by the force of the current into the Sea of Okhotsk, and then in the course of between ten or fifteen years in salt water becomes strong enough to migrate upstream, back to where it came from in the lower and middle Amur to spawn. A kaluga can weigh up to a tonne, it is a cunning predator and a threat to every other species in the river, including ducks, frogs and rodents, and is prized by the peoples on both sides of the border for its valuable caviar. As it was the end of the spawning season, we hoped to taste this delicacy, but were unsuccessful in that endeavour.

Along the way we also kept an eye out for the dwellings of the locals – the Oroch and Kilen Goldes. We went ashore on both the Russian and Chinese side, collecting many interesting ethnographic objects.

I mentioned previously the drinking orgies of the Mongols and Buryats, and it was during this part of our journey we encountered yet another variant of the natives' debauchery, practised this time by the Chinese Daurs, who after a long and arduous hunting season by the upper and middle course of the Amur have traditionally stayed at the dwellings of the locals, who waste no time in serving them millet wine in tubes of fish bladder; we tasted this concoction ourselves. When the Daur people drink it, they forget all about the hard slog in the forests, no longer fear food shortages next spring, and let themselves go completely, selling their hard-earned riches – sable and other leather goods – for next to nothing to the scoundrels who have plied them with drink. We heard that this is an annual occurrence, year in, year out.

In Radeffka, we sold the boat, with a heavy heart, and went aboard yet another river steamer that would take us further downriver to Khabarovsk. On board this ship, we met several other adventurers, amongst them two French collectors working for Deyrolle in Paris, Europe's most prominent taxidermist at the time. We had ourselves – via

Staudinger – sent some items there. The Frenchmen were travelling together with a Danish researcher engaged in documenting the languages of the region. There were also three Americans amongst the passengers, all dressed in sand-coloured khakis. They claimed to be big-game hunters, hunting purely for sport, mainly bears and wolves, but appeared more interested in drinking bourbon and laughing at something or other, presumably they were wealthy. But it was not possible to engage them in conversation to any great degree, since they did not speak any other language but their own.

Still, everyone was pleasant, and we were able to spend a few enjoyable days sharing our experiences with like-minded people. We benefited greatly from the company of the Frenchmen, who in addition to their activities in collecting had developed a system of teaching in French schools and universities, with charts and illustrations of all types of fauna, flora and natural phenomena. The idea was to bring the museums to the people, they said. More than half of their incomes already stemmed from this pedagogical activity. They also wrote articles for textbooks and encyclopaedias, and for a prominent newspaper now and then.

They had in their possession a modern photographic apparatus, a so-called "Eastman camera", which used not glass plates but roll film, and which they demonstrated for us. They had also taken some interesting pictures of trees and rock formations, as well as of Golde *fanser* and a freshly shot Asian black bear. But already back then we realised that it would be decades before the apparatus was sophisticated enough to capture a specimen in motion, not to mention sufficiently robust to withstand the rigours of the field, such as cold, rain and sand.

*

We said our farewells to the party in Khabarovsk and went aboard yet another steamer. This carried us up the Ussuri to Kozlovska, and from there we went down to the Suchan region, where we took up lodging in a dilapidated log house with the intention of wintering there; indeed, we would stay in the area for the next two years.

We spent the autumn preparing and packing the approximately four thousand butterflies and beetles we had amassed during the year, before we set about registering and capturing the winter species.

Again, we encountered tigers, but first a few words about the leopard (*Panthera pardus orientalis*), because we acquired two specimens of this rare animal in the late autumn of that year, one weighing more than forty kilos with a wonderful two-layered almost flame-like winter pelt.

The males can be up to a metre and a half in length; they are yellowish red with black spots, and hunt in the same terrain as the tiger, for the same prey, so it is a mystery to me how they can co-exist. We made several attempts to catch one alive, using traps, but to no avail. The specimens we got the better of with firearms were both males, one somewhat younger than the other; the contents of their stomachs indicated they had not eaten in a while, and this is deer terrain. Later, when I spoke to Russian hunters about these remarkable animals, I had the impression that they were scarcely aware of them, or at least were not very interested in them, it really was all about the tiger.

The tiger has migrated northwards along the temperate coast and has come by way of Korea over to the area surrounding the source of the Ussuri. This great cat is also found along the Suifun, and its adjacent tributaries, with the exception of a few districts with a notable lack of wildlife. Neither is it rare in the area around the River Bureya or the

Khingan Mountains north-west of the Amur. It prefers vast pine forests, where the pine cones attract wild boar, which the tiger can pursue for miles and miles when it detects their scent. It will initially try to take a young animal or a sow, seeking to steer clear of the large hogs.

One tiger we shot that winter showed clear signs of having fought just such a male boar. He had a gaping wound, some sixteen centimetres long, down his chest, and we registered several deep cuts with torn sinew on his right hind leg. Since the tiger could easily reach all these wounds with his tongue, he could no doubt have hastened the healing process, but when we examined his stomach contents, we found only undigested grass and leaves, which could indicate that the wounds had made it difficult – if not impossible – to hunt.

57

The following spring, we moved to the highlands south of Suchan, remaining there throughout the summer. This is a volcanic area, with fertile, green valleys, mountainsides sliced by wooded ravines, and above them steep mountains reaching skywards.

After just a few days we found the coveted butterfly Sericinus var. telemachus, yet another new species, a swallowtail. The area was so rich in both butterflies and moths that over summer and autumn we could delight in a bounty of more than eight hundred specimens, comprising both those we bred ourselves and those captured.

I also managed to catch the large Catocala doerriesi moth, which Staudinger later named after us. On top of everything else, we got hold of a very interesting bird, an owl that no scientist had either seen or heard of previously, an impressive strigiform that would in time be called the large fish owl. It is bigger than the eagle owl and was also named after us: Bubo blakistoni doerriesi (later changed to Ketupa b. d.).

To our great delight, we again found several variants of the rare Parnassius, the species our father had shown us drawings of in childhood. This beautiful butterfly suddenly appeared right in front of me, I only had eyes for it – had I yet another Parnassius nomion in the net!? But as I held the incredible creature up in the sunlight to fully savour the sight of it, I found myself staring straight at the head of a tiger on a rocky outcrop above me. I was stunned, to put it mildly, but curiously enough managed to collect myself, and calmly packed my nomion away.

Whilst I did so, the tiger kept his eyes firmly on the net. It probably was not hungry. I moved slowly backwards, without letting the beast out of my sight and resumed my activity thirty metres away. But I found no more Parnassius that day. We would, however, have luck on our side later, as though some barrier had been broken with this find. And our Parnassius can still be admired in many museums in Europe and Asia, described by Staudinger.

58

We worked systematically through yet another winter and had to face the fact that Edmund was not quite like Friedrich and me after all. In the summertime, he was the most tenacious member of our expedition, never complaining about hardships, neither lack of sleep nor workload. But he had problems with the cold, possibly as a consequence of all the years in the Amazon, and was unable to work outdoors when the thermometer sank below minus twenty degrees, not to mention when it neared minus forty, at which point his fingers stiffened. This was not due to any lack of willpower, he simply suffered from frostbite sooner than we did.

The problem was solved by allowing him to work indoors, preparing and logging, in the hardest periods, and he was second to none at this – one of his masterpieces is an arrangement with a total of forty-four hummingbirds he brought from the Amazon, mounted on a little tree, a breathtaking creation that is still in the family's possession and is perhaps our most spectacular trophy.

At the end of spring, our second in the region, we were again so laden that we decided to travel to Vladivostok to have the collection loaded aboard a German steamship we had heard was leaving for Europe the following week.

But whilst we were at the chamber of commerce, busy organising the packing and the formalities regarding the shipment, Edmund mumbled something about wanting to go along on the voyage, to travel home and assist our father in the job of selling the haul.

It came as a great surprise to us – Father managed the task perfectly well, even though now and then certain peculiarities might arise, like when he was unwilling to hand over particular objects to scientists or institutions he lacked confidence in.

Neither had Edmund complained about anything, apart from the cold, on our travels, so he realised he would have to dish up a better explanation. Finally, he told us that during his stay at home he had applied for a position as a taxidermist at the Umlauffsches Museum in Hamburg and had now in Vladivostok received a telegram stating the position was his. There was little else we could do but wish him all the best.

59

We bade farewell to our little brother at the docks in Vladivostok. Henry and I soon equipped ourselves for a new expedition and went north towards the Khekhtsir Ridge. But game turned out to be scarce at that time of year, so after a few days we decided we would rather spend the last month of the summer trying to find out more about the fate of the Russian criminals in the katorga, and perhaps take a closer look at the island of Sakhalin, practically uncharted territory from a scientific viewpoint, though the reptile population had to an extent been surveyed and presented in a Russian study a few years previously.

We proceeded to Khabarovsk and boarded a river steamer that over the course of three peaceful days took us roughly a thousand miles down the Amur, to the town of Nikolaevsk by the Sea of Okhotsk, arriving in the middle of September.

Thanks to a letter of recommendation from Moscow we received assistance from the Governor-General of eastern Siberia, Count Muravev (*muravey* means "ant", incidentally), who resided here. Muravev put us in contact with the captain of a cargo ship heading to Sakhalin, an ornery, taciturn man who, after a little humming and hawing, agreed to allow us aboard. The fact we could produce documentation proving we were men of science no doubt made things easier – moreover, we could pay.

Sakhalin is twice the area of Denmark in size and stretches along the coastline of eastern Siberia from La Pérouse Strait to the mouth of the Amur, separated from the mainland by the so-called Strait of Tartary, which in the north is no wider than thirty-five nautical miles.

Most of the prisoners are, as mentioned previously, marched here on foot, with some recourse to river boat. But several times a year the Dobrevolne shipping line also transported prisoners on their large steamships, sailing under a fluttering black flag across the Black Sea, through the Bosporus and Suez, and over the Indian Ocean and the South and East China seas.

The entire lower decks of these ships were loaded with iron cages, where hard-bitten criminals and murderers had to lie in chains for the whole voyage. As they reached the tropics they would encounter their first sufferings, the terrible heat below deck driving them out of their minds, many becoming ill and dying before they reached their destination. On Sakhalin they were lined up and freed from their shackles, which were then thrown into the sea, something of a ritual, we were told. Presumably it signified that there was no way back from there, even if they managed to escape and make it to the mainland. Siberia is too great and man too small.

At a harbour called Due, about halfway down the island's west coast, the ship docked to load coal, and the captain granted us six hours at our disposal. We went ashore and what should we spot but a host of discarded leg irons on the beach, which we were told were left by the hundred and fifty hardened criminals who had recently arrived from Odessa.

From the first hill we walked up we had a view of the entire little town, and of one of the prisons, large, spacious halls with open entrances at either end, probably to allow for some form of air circulation. These buildings were constructed of solid logs and situated around an enormous yard, with a four-metre-high plank wall securing the perimeter.

We also wished to take a look inside, so we walked down and knocked at the main gate. A soldier opened, and after speaking to us, sent for an official by the name of Baerle, who examined our papers and without further ado offered to show us around.

We crossed the open square and were led into a clerk's office. The friendly Herr Baerle, who by the way spoke excellent German, first offered us a cup of tea and then called in an oddly dressed gentleman and gave him some orders. The man bowed and scraped in a subservient manner, and when he was sent away again, Baerle asked if we had noticed anything in particular about him.

We replied that we had not, apart from his strange apparel, which made him look almost like an actor at a carnival.

Baerle told us that the man had murdered his own brother, a reigning king. We looked at one another, not understanding what he meant, whether it was intended as a joke, or if the fellow in question was mad, and we were left with no answer, only an enigmatic smile.

After we had drunk our tea, he brought us on a tour of the large halls where the prisoners were working. Except for murderers, all were allowed to practise their own professions. There were watchmakers, shoemakers, gunsmiths, and carpenters making the most charming jewellery boxes out of birch, indeed, they produced all manner of furniture and decor for cottages and houses, goods that would be shipped to Europe and sold, it seemed to be a very lucrative arrangement for the state.

The prisoners worked unsupervised and did not appear to be bored or suffer from want. We spoke to several of them, and they told us that both their treatment and the board provided were good. The dormitories were right next to the workshops, bunk beds, three or four beds high. We also observed that when the soldier on duty at the main gate had to answer the call of nature, he would give one of the prisoners a shout, hand over his loaded weapon, and ask him to stand guard in the meantime.

After our thorough look around, Baerle placed his own wagon at our disposal, including a coachman, a former prisoner we learned, now employed at the facility. He drove us approximately twelve versts southwards along the beach to the next settlement.

Every inhabitant there was a settler, that is to say a former inmate, who after serving their sentences lived as free men, albeit with the not inconsiderable constraint of never again setting foot on European soil, a policy that would contribute to the colonisation of eastern Siberia.

There were men, women and children, as in any community, served by a school and a small church. We spoke to several of them and did not register any unusual hardship or need here either. But some rather odd quirks were exhibited that ought to have aroused our suspicions: when we asked an elderly man his name, he answered, Nepomnyashchiy. And the next person we met said the same. Nepomnyashchi means "don't remember". A third man we encountered claimed he was called Vosemdesyatgod, meaning "eighty years", and he was not even forty. It may have been that they were all illiterate. Or had been there so long that they could neither recall what their names were or where they came from. They had a taciturn and apathetic way about them that we had not noticed in other settlers. We approached a fourth man, and when he also gave his name as Nepomnyashchi, we were determined to get to the bottom of the matter, but we did not get very far before the coachman intervened, declaring it was time to go.

He drove us back to the prison camp, where we were informed that Baerle was otherwise occupied but that the ship was ready to set sail. We went aboard, sailing further south along the west coast of the island, left with the impression that the reputation for poor treatment of prisoners seemed at odds with what we had seen. At any rate, we had found the conditions in Due passably humane. But there was something strange about the island, and perhaps the notorious mines were hidden from us – it would be remiss of me not to mention that we were not allowed go ashore anywhere else but the appointed harbour.

Consequently, we were denied the opportunity of paying a visit to the Ainu, a people in danger of dying out, according to Captain Hoeck, who had told us there were now only eight hundred left on Sakhalin. They were tenacious people locked in an admirable, eternal struggle against the forces of nature. They lived mainly by hunting and fishing. Most of their clothing they made from sealskins, sewn together with nettle fibre, which they processed on primitive looms. They also sewed coats from puffin skins, wearing them with the plumage on the inside, and they loved to adorn their garments with the splendid bills and crests of the bird. Fatal diseases, including leprosy, were widespread amongst them and their faces bore the unmistakable signs of it, according to Hoeck.

Hoeck had previously sold me a collection of ethnographic objects from this very people, which, together with what he and the Koryak Samuel had given me, can be found today in the Museum of Ethnology in Hamburg. And here is a little anecdote in connection with that:

I had valued Hoeck's and Samuel's pieces at four thousand marks. But the people at the museum acted miserly and wanted to haggle. A friend of my father – a wealthy idealist – got to hear of this, gave me the sum I was asking for, and donated the pieces to the museum. But he passed away shortly afterwards and this four thousand marks was found to be missing from his estate. A court case ensued, and the upshot was that the museum had to reimburse the beneficiaries of the will for the whole amount; I could not help but gloat inwardly when I heard about the matter.

We enjoyed a peaceful eight-day voyage southward off Sakhalin, an island I can only describe as monumental, with flat, wet and cold tundra in the north, then low, gentle slopes and rising hills the further south one goes, with virgin forests, rivers and mountains that we would gladly have taken a closer look at.

But we were not permitted to go ashore, despite there being numerous places to moor, and the fact that the ship was equipped with two small boats. This was contrary to our nature, and we repeatedly offered our reticent captain money; we had weapons and equipment, enough provisions to last at least three weeks, and we would have managed to make it back to the mainland under our own steam.

But the man was peculiar for a Russian in that he was completely incorruptible. Henry suggested threatening him at gunpoint, but I thought that would be going a bit far with "the ox", as we had begun calling him. We interpreted his intractability as evidence he was acting according to the express orders of Governor Muravev in Nikolayevsk, something we would later confirm. All we could do was sail on to Vladivostok thinking of what might have been.

60

To shake off the feeling of disappointment, we made our stay with Gammenthaler as short as possible and left for the Chimochhae, a river emptying into Ussuri Bay, where the bird migration south was under way. Here we made every effort to get hold of specimens of species we might previously have overlooked. And we successfully registered some new ones.

While Henry stayed behind to hunt birds of the forest and shore, I travelled eighty versts up to the mountains west of the River Suchan to chart the nesting grounds of the Steller's sea eagle (*Haliaeetus pelagicus*), the largest and most beautiful eagle in Asia, the species Wanka and I had caught glimpses of on Askold.

And this journey was a success: I registered both fledglings and fully-grown examples of three species of eagle in all. But the hunt for the black and white Pelagicus had to be put on hold until winter, when we might have a chance of acquiring some specimens in their winter plumage.

I was ready to make my return trip when halfway down the wooded side of a valley I met some Manchurians sitting around a fire making tea, they were beekeepers on their way to Khabarovsk to sell their wares. In the course of our conversation, they told me of a special breed of goat living in the Sjantalase Range, also pointing out two places on my map.

I thus put off my return, riding even further south instead, and stood two days later at the foot of the massif marked on the map, a precipitous block, a shocking sight: rising out of the otherwise autumnal forest stood a stark white molar of a mountain, a predator's fang of shiny, white rock. I searched back and forth at the base, without seeing hide nor hair of the goats.

But I could not just give up and leave, so I set up camp, slept under some furs, and began climbing the next morning towards the other spot indicated on the map, leaving the horse behind.

It was not overwhelmingly steep to start with. But just over an hour later I was standing at the foot of yet another massif, considerably steeper. However, a solution presented itself, in the form of a narrow gully which brought me some four hundred feet higher, with the help of some dwarf oaks I could hold on to. After about two hours I reached the top, where it was possible to continue along a narrow ridge.

At some points, this ridge was no more than two or three feet wide, consisting of only porous pebbles, eroded by snow, ice and wind, with no vegetation. In other places I had to inch my way along, mindful of a drop of more than a thousand feet to my left, with the bottom hoving in and out of view as raggedy clouds scudded by. At the time I was not dizzy in the slightest – now I can hardly bear to think about it.

Finally, I reached the gentler slope where the goats were supposed to reside but there was no sign of them. I zig-zagged slowly back and forth across the strange sloping "roof" for a time, but found neither tracks nor excrement, so when it also started pouring with rain, I decided to go back.

On the return journey along the narrow ridge, I met two bewildered deer. Up here? I thought. I was able to shoot one, but it was not possible to carry the hundred-and-forty-pound carcass, so after disembowelling it, I threw it down. And after having survived the descent, which proved even more dramatic than the ascent, not least because of the persistent rain, I found my kill at the foot of the mountains, battered and scraped, its legs broken in several places.

I tied the animal across the horse and rode on, continuing down.

Along the way I was crossing a narrow hollow when suddenly a bear stood facing me. It was still raining torrentially. I raised my rifle, but the reins were resting on my arms, and as I was about to fire, the horse tossed his head, pulling at them and causing me to miss. The bear disappeared. I could, in other words, report to Henry upon my return a trip marked by fluctuations of fortune, but the main objective had been accomplished: I knew where the Steller's sea eagles were located.

61

At the end of October, we again turned our attention to beasts of prey. We prepared, amongst others, another leopard. We had happened on this particular specimen when it had just killed a fawn, and my dog managed to chase it up a tree. Unfortunately, the rare animal was not yet in its winter coat.

Furthermore, we shot two bears, one brown bear and a completely black variant of the behringiana. In the mountain forests we also killed six specimens of the grey wildcat, which can grow to more than a metre long, and was rare in those parts. In winters with heavy snowfall, this powerful creature can venture into settlements to take poultry. On the Sidimi peninsula, Henry shot one specimen of the somewhat smaller red species (*Felis microtis*), whose actual home is in Korea. We very seldom saw lynxes and did not shoot any.

By the River Maicha I downed a male wolverine (*Gulo sibiricus*). Sables were nowhere to be found, but there were on the other hand many stoats, martens, badgers and squirrels, the latter sporting a fantastic grey-red winter coat, called vair, which was highly sought after amongst the natives.

The raccoon dog was also common. It is very trusting, and if caught unawares while foraging, it does not even consider running away, but readily takes the time to sniff at the hunter's foot before ambling off, with a backward glance, as if wondering: what in the world was that creature?

On rare occasions, we also met a flying squirrel (*Pteromys volans*). These small creatures subsist in winter mainly on the cones of Swiss pines and birch buds. Earlier in the year I had been so fortunate as to stumble upon the dwelling of one of these intriguing species, in an abandoned woodpecker hole, about two metres above the ground. When I knocked upon the tree trunk, in the hope of finding a woodpecker nest, a sweet little silvery grey head popped out, its big, dark eyes filling almost its entire face. I withdrew cautiously, the head disappeared, and the animal was free to resume her maternal duties.

In the dense spruce and deciduous forests by the River Chimochhae we often encountered the large yellow-throated marten, a brave and dogged creature, and the great enemy of the roe deer. When a human approaches, it will usually raise itself on its hind legs, climb up a tree and jump from branch to branch to get away.

We had already secured several fine specimens of the species, when on a narrow ridge I caught sight of a sea eagle atop the carcass of a roe deer leisurely filling its stomach with meat. It took flight and disappeared as I drew closer. But the head of a yellow-throated marten suddenly popped up from inside the carcass and looked anxiously around. I took down the rogue with a well-aimed shot. Or so I thought. Because when I grabbed it by the tail to put it in my sack, it spun quickly around and clung to me in a desperate attempt to bite my throat, which is how it kills its quarry.

I just about managed to get a stranglehold on the animal and choke it to death. After placing it in the sack, I followed the tracks of the dead deer, and could ascertain that it had managed to make it about fifteen paces with the marten on its neck before collapsing.

62

Late in November, I decided to accompany six Russian woodsmen up along the River Maicha in the area between Amur Bay and Ussuri Bay, a mountainous region with an abundance of deer. The idea was to hunt game for myself and Henry, as well as for the impoverished Russians we were sharing a house with at the time – several of the families were suffering privations, and winter had scarcely begun.

I measured the temperature, both day and night, at between fifteen and twenty below zero. We had no tent, and the woodsmen did not think it was worth building a log house for just two weeks, but rather spent every hour felling timber, which incidentally was to be sold to a Cossack garrison with plans to expand. So we sat around the fire each night, drinking tea, chatting, puffing on our pipes – and freezing.

Amongst the men was a hunter, about fifty years of age, with a weather-beaten face marked by old scars. I asked how he had come by them and was told that he had been out with a companion when he had stumbled upon a she-bear with cubs. He had fired a shot, but missed, and the she-bear had thrown herself on him. Luckily, his companion heard his screams, arrived on the scene and shot her through the ear.

"And this friend," the hunter continued, "who saved my life thirty years ago, was himself killed by a tiger, or a bear, we don't know for certain, because when we found him – some ravens led us to the spot – only his skull remained, along with a few bones. He was identified thanks to an old gold coin that he always kept in his right shoe, to bribe the devil with, in case he should wake up in hell. And now it's mine!"

He held the shiny coin up triumphantly between two frozen fingers and, with a broad grin, said, "Because what need does he have for it for in heaven?"

We wrapped ourselves in furs and blankets and stretched our feet out towards the campfire. I lay between the enormous roots of a metre-thick pine. In this cold there was no chance of getting much sleep, so we were happy until every time the starry sky began to grow pale.

The hunting was terrible in the first week, we had to live on dry bread and tea, and morale deteriorated as everyone grew increasingly testy, so I was on the verge of calling off the entire expedition when I finally got an old hind in my sights. Less than an hour later, we were sitting around a steaming pot eating ourselves headily full: salted broth, meat, fat and soup as well as the ever-present Russian bread I never got enough of. I even dug up a few herbs from the snow to season the glorious dish and can hardly recall a more wonderful meal.

The following week was even better, the Russians were busy felling trees from morning to night, and I killed four magnificent deer. On a remote low-lying mountain range, I also brought down an eight-tined buck. On my way back to the camp that day I was passing through a narrow valley – unsuspecting and with the happy heart of the hunter – when a tiger appeared thirty paces ahead, a magnificent male.

Unfortunately, darkness was falling, so I could only just discern its outline. It no doubt saw me too and considered attacking but declined to do me that favour. All the same I fired a couple of shots. The dark form made a long leap down into a hollow and disappeared. Approaching cautiously, I came across the fresh remains of a raccoon dog in the snow, flesh, blood and bones, the tiger's interrupted meal, and I tried to find a blood trail from the cat, but had to concede that I had probably missed, and decided to put off my pursuit until the next day, making use of the tracks in the snow.

But when I returned to the camp, the Russians, standing lined up like soldiers, declared themselves finished with the work, enough was enough, the sleds were already packed, and all of them gave me an accusing look when they saw my hesitation. I took it lightly, quickly abandoned my dream of a tiger, and loaded the deer onto the sled, and we made our way back to the warm parlours of the settlement, where the families were beside themselves with joy over the supply of meat. Sometimes food and warmth are more important than even a tiger.

63

By the end of the year, we could at last begin preparations for the long-awaited Steller's sea eagle hunt. We packed two sleighs with the bare essentials, including two large bags of black bread, tea and sugar. Our journey took us first north along the coast, and then inland towards the Sjantalase range, where the ascent could begin. At six in the evening, on December 31, after travelling continuously uphill for sixty-five versts, we reached the mountain range in its magnificent winter dress. It was here I had registered the large birds of prey the previous autumn. A dilapidated log house gave us some shelter against the winter weather.

We got a good night's sleep and then made a few brief trips outside to map the terrain the next day, as well as killing a couple of deer for provisions. When we got a big enough fire going in the rusty stove, it was actually quite pleasant in the doleful house.

The following morning, Henry and I went our separate ways – once again we were dividing the area between us – and I headed up to higher ground. I discovered intersecting deer tracks at the foot of a steep rock-face. So as not to ruin the trail, I moved twenty paces back and lit a pipe to determine the wind direction. Fortunately, the breeze was blowing downslope. I remained standing, looking up at the sky for the long-awaited eagles, but there was nothing to see.

I had hardly finished my pipe when I noticed movement and raised the rifle to my cheek. The shot rang out like a howl through the white landscape, and a deer of all of one hundred and ninety pounds lay dead in the blinding white snow, just as I planned. Desirable carrion for birds of prey.

I wanted them unblemished by gunshot wounds, so I poisoned the carcass with strychnine and withdrew back downhill, not to return for four days, sleeping in a crude tent I constructed of canvas and birch. I did not dare light a fire, so time passed slowly.

Early on the morning of the fourth day, I set out uphill, and it is not possible to describe the weight of expectation I felt. A profound calm lay over the snow-covered woods, not a birdcall to be heard nor any movement to be seen. The landscape seemed completely dead. I only crossed wolf tracks twice. Eventually I took up a position forty or fifty metres from the scene of the kill.

Soon after, two ravens took off from the carcass. One let out a short squawk, hit the snow headfirst, and lay there struggling to move, while the other tottered out of my field of vision. I approached the almost entirely consumed deer – and what a sight! Not in my wildest imaginings had I dared to dream of this: a grand total of thirteen birds of prey lay strewn around the battlefield. Amongst them, four marvellous, old Steller's sea eagles, two males and two females. The rest were golden eagles and ospreys. I circled the carcass at a distance and also found two old wolves, a fox, some blue jays, a few ravens and two stoats.

A haul such as this demanded to be celebrated, but how? I must admit

I did not know what else to do but take off my fur hat and throw it in the air like an idiot, then light a pipe, which had never tasted better.

Four fantastic Pelagicus. These eagles are tigers of the sky, of flesh and blood. Even after I had removed the entrails, there was barely enough room in the two backpacks, both woven from strips of deerskin in the Oroch fashion and thus highly flexible.

I would almost call these birds sailors – no other creature of the same weight can hold itself light as a feather in the sky. The black and white plumage, the powerful yellow beak, the huge yellow feet and the grey, dagger-like talons, worthy of a king of the wild. These are the biggest eagles in the world, with a wingspan of more than two and half metres, and live only here, on Kamchatka and Sakhalin, and possibly on Hokkaido in the winter.

I was almost finished with packing when I heard the distinct sound of wingbeats. Out from over the closest peak soared yet another Pelagicus, which attempted, as soon as it saw me, to fly away again with its characteristic paddling movements. I grabbed hold of the shotgun and fired both barrels simultaneously, and down sailed the fifth Pelagicus with wings outspread.

This day of hunting, in addition to bringing in a tidy sum for us, was one of the most meaningful in my life, because of the absence of these splendid eagles in most European museums and because they had occupied a place in my mind since my first trip to Askold, when Wanka and I could only admire them from afar.

It was not possible to move the entire haul in one go, so I dragged the first pack about one verst down the mountain, returned and fetched the other and brought it a verst past the first, depositing it there, before retracing my steps to collect the first, threading a laborious backstitch through the night to our ramshackle dwelling.

But there was no sign of Henry, just a note saying he had given up and gone back to Chimochhae, having not sighted a single Pelagicus.

I slept late, went down to the nearest settlement and hired four horses, two sleds and a driver! We rolled the eagles up in blankets, loaded them on the sleds and drove towards Chimochhae, where two days later I again met my brother. Neither he nor I had words for the haul, but he did manage to splutter:

"Unbelievable."

We have never been more meticulous in preparing specimens for stuffing. And when the work was done, I did not place the treasures in a trunk as usual, but in my sturdy suitcase, with mountings and two locks, and ensured that from then on it barely left my sight.

64

Over our years spent in Siberia – and by now there had been many – we had got so close to the animals that at times we could feel at one with them. Situations constantly arose in which emotion threatened to overshadow both our hunting instincts and scientific dispositions. I want to mention four episodes in particular, all related to birds and, as though ordained by fate, occurring in the year which commenced with the killing of the eagles.

In March or April, we caught some waders, including some species of snipe amongst them (*Totanus* and *Tringa*), who alight here in large flocks to rest on their way to their breeding grounds in the north. Amongst the multitude of Tringa, we also found the rare shoveler (*Anas clypeata*), which nests on Kamchatka, and obtained five specimens.

But one day a dark cloud flew over us at an incredible speed.

"What manner of birds are they?"

We sought cover in the thicket, hoping more might show up. And not long after, a new flock, just as closely packed, appeared. We each fired, both using the finest pellets we had, and from what we could make out, hit three birds. But none of them fell to the ground, just continued with wings close to their bodies for three or four hundred metres and disappeared into the forest. And they were nowhere to be found, not even with the help of outstanding Golde dogs. We realised it was impossible to shoot these birds from the side or from behind, but all the same we did manage to bring down almost twenty specimens. It was the strangest hunt I have taken part in. They were large, heavy swallows, resembling house martins, but of a species utterly unknown to us, definitely something for Bolau!

However, later on, the entire collection went missing, either in Vladivostok or en route to Europe, and we never encountered the species again, nor did I make any drawings of them; moreover, I was rather careless in my descriptions, so to this day we have been unable to find out exactly the type of bird in question. So many unfortunate circumstances around one find is something a collector should not experience more than once.

Early one morning, we were in a swampy area, surrounded by heavy, cold fog, before the sun eventually broke through. We had built some hides from various shrubs and bushes, and our presence there at precisely this time of day had been carefully calculated.

First, several flocks of geese flew over us. Then we heard cranes (*Grus viridirostris*) but could not see them. We sat with shotguns at the ready throughout the rest of the morning, until another crane finally appeared in the sky, a female. As cranes fly so high, we were using heavier shot. When the bird was hit, she let her legs dangle straight down and sailed slowly to earth. Thirty metres behind her, however, a male flew into view, and as the female dived, he suddenly adjusted and soared upwards in a diagonal direction.

We let the dog seek out the female, and as I lifted our prey up to examine her more closely, I heard a commotion in the air above, and down came the male crashing to earth, wings dangling, dying on impact as his beak bore deep into the marsh.

We prepared the birds, and while the female was peppered with shot, the male was not wounded at all.

So what did he die from?

I dissected his brain and discovered bleeding, so I presume he must have had a stroke when he saw his partner lying dead in the swamp.

In early summer, I fired at two mute swans. The pen lay dead, but on a nest. If I had known she was atop two eggs I would never have fired. The cob immediately took flight and disappeared. But when I returned about ten or eleven days later to see if he had taken over the incubation, he was also lying dead beside the nest. Upon later close examination of his stomach contents, I was able to ascertain that he had not eaten since the pen died. He had most likely starved to death from grief.

By the River Maicha I encountered three Oriental storks (*Ciconia boyciana*) strolling solemnly around in the wet marshlands. I sneaked closer and lay down on a slight mound with a clear line of sight. But I could still only make out their heads, plus a little of their necks now and then. At a distance of about one hundred and fifty metres, and only equipped with a rifle, it was important to take very careful aim. I fired at the chest of the one closest and the bird collapsed to the ground. The others were clearly agitated, but quickly calmed down. I shot a second the same way, and not long after claimed a third of these fantastic storks, with their snow-white plumage, black beaks and red legs.

One can kill a butterfly between one's thumb and forefinger, by simply squeezing it until the keratin armour cracks, or by placing it in a jar of potassium cyanide, which makes short work of it. And in those cases, we did not have the same sense of killing as when we shot birds and deer, not to mention tigers and eagles. It is, of course, because butterflies are smaller and have a minuscule nervous system and blood system, thus death is instantaneous. But beneath a magnifying glass and a microscope no species are lesser than any other, and this caused us to become increasingly contemplative. There was, on the whole, plenty in nature to make us reflect more and more as time went on – I think I would have to say that the longer we lived in the wilderness, the more often I would recall our father's words about only the incomprehensible being worth pursuing.

65

We saddled the horses, stocked up with enough bread and oats for six days, and set off one morning at dawn, reaching the Paide Mountains after an eight-hour ride. There we entered a narrow valley, on the lookout for an abandoned earth lodge we had got wind of. We found the dwelling in an idyllic setting, beside a fast-flowing stream. The roof had collapsed on the bunks, which were covered in rotten straw, but we soon repaired the damage, gathered some wood for the night and lit a fire.

A bear ambled past, looked at the flames, and stopped to sniff for a moment, before walking slowly on. The leaves fell from the trees like tiny blessings. We had duck leg, bread and tea, and the night looked like it would be a cold one, so we pulled our wolf pelts tight around our shoulders, smoked yet another pipe and made plans for the next day, before we turned in for the night in the rotten lodge to dream ourselves away, as Mother used to say.

But I cannot have slept more than a quarter of an hour when the mattress beneath me seemed to come to life. There was an undulating, gentle rocking motion, so I called out to Henry to wake him up, and he too discovered similar movement beneath him.

A true man of the forest is always apprehensive. That feeling is probably his most important asset, so we jumped up immediately, lit a candle and pulled off the straw. And what a sight! No fewer than forty small, medium-sized, and metre-long pit vipers (*Ancistrodon blomhoffi*) lay in the weak light, wriggling before our incredulous eyes. They had settled down for the winter, only to be disturbed in their hibernation. But how had they all come together here, a species we otherwise only ever saw alone and at great distances from one another – and so equally distributed on two beds?

As soon as it was light, we fed the horses a bucket of soggy black bread and a little hay, and went hunting, after both agreeing to return when darkness fell.

Henry chose the north side of a valley with dense pine forest, where we had heard some smaller species of marten might be found, whilst I struck out for the mixed forest south of our camp. I heard shots from the other side but did not give it much thought. I downed a yellow-throated marten and a raccoon dog, found a tree with honey and was back at the camp when darkness fell as arranged.

But Henry was nowhere to be seen.

I waited an hour, but he did not arrive. There was nothing else for it but to head back to where I had heard shots earlier. I returned to the spot, fired our prearranged signal of seven shots, but heard nothing in response. As it was now completely dark and I was without a dog, I could not continue to search. Upset, I returned to camp, took care of the horses, boiled some tea, tended the fire and waited for morning.

Dawn broke, and from then until dusk, I searched, crisscrossing the rugged mountain terrain, without becoming any the wiser. A new and even longer night followed. The third day was also spent on a fruitless search. In the late afternoon I gave up, saddled my horse and rode to the nearest village, called on a hetman I knew and asked for twelve Cossacks to help me look. We had to find my brother, dead or alive.

He recognised the gravity of the situation and we set out immediately, with dogs, riding single file in silence southwards along a barely visible trail next to the sea. Quivering strips of silver moonlight played across the waves. A flock of shorebirds took flight, alighting again a few hundred metres away, to resume sleeping with their heads tucked under their wings.

I could already glimpse the outline of the Paide Mountains when one of the Cossacks drew my attention to a figure tottering towards us along the path. In itself, not a rarity, even out there in the wilderness, it could be a hunter, anyone at all. And it was a hunter – it was my brother Henry, whom I had not seen in more than three days and presumed dead, but who now fell into our arms, utterly exhausted and half-perished from hunger. He said he had been stalking some wild boar and had simply been unable to find his way back to the lodge.

He was more than a little ashamed. As far as I remember this was the only time he lost his way in all the years we were in Siberia. The snakes in the earth lodge came to mind, seemingly equipped with an unerring compass, but I thought better of mentioning it. He was no doubt put in mind of them himself, and he later touched upon how his error in navigation had in no way detracted from the draw he felt to this country, in case I was to suppose such a thing, and neither had it rendered him more fearful nor estranged from it, quite the contrary. It is not possible to explore Siberia completely, as Father had impressed upon us about butterflies, or as the man had told the prisoners on Sakhalin: Siberia is too big and man too small.

66

It was late September, and the evergreen spruce grew ever darker against the deciduous forest, a display of colour without equal blazed in the brilliant sunshine, announcing a season that – as usual – was all too quickly nearing its end, the Siberian autumn. The large, reddish-brown, serrated leaves of the Mongolian oak, the pale yellow foliage on both species of linden tree, elms turning light brown, the ash and the Amur cork tree still standing in shiny dark green.

The leaves of the walnut tree had become crumbled and brown. White and black birch were lit up in the most beautiful yellow hues, whilst the large, round leaves of the poplar resembled ripe apples. Overwhelming beauty, no matter where we looked.

Although most of the migratory birds had set off southwards, some species still gave life to the forest, not least an old black woodpecker who had become a pure housebird here by the earth lodge (the snakes were still sleeping inside and we outside), a tireless worker who would usually prefer the darkest thicket but had strayed into the deciduous forest to chip at the roots of dead birch trees, hunting for larvae that it retrieved with its long, spiny tongue, before it flew over to a dead, branchless poplar trunk whose life had ended in the last forest fire, standing like a black colossus in the young forest, with the old black woodpecker atop it, hammering away with its familiar drumming sound, audible for miles around: what a life we lived!

It was October 22, and once more our collection had grown so vast that we had to get it home. We had been on the move on this expedition for more than six years, the first three with Edmund. Again, we decided to deliver our treasures personally, Henry somewhat hesitantly, as he would have rather spent the winter with Captain Hoeck on Sidimi again, but he had also begun toying with the idea of setting up a business in Hamburg, a taxidermy shop, and having someone to run it for him so he could continue with the hunter's life in Siberia, as a supplier of raw materials of a sort. Besides, it was probably a good idea to offer the family some reassurance again, we both remembered how sombre Mother had been last time we left, and we were not getting any younger.

We packed nine chests. The bird collection alone consisted of more than a thousand specimens, amongst them some very rare species. (However, as mentioned: the mysterious swallows disappeared, either in Vladivostok or somewhere else along the way!) We had also discovered a new, small species of woodpecker and had secured twenty examples. It was later given the name Ingipicus doerriesi, and again I think we have Bolau to thank for that.

On October 30, 1895, we went aboard a Russian steamer, reaching Odessa a month and a half later. From there we took a train, arriving home late in December.

67

As usual the welcome was overwhelming. Once more we placed bell jars with butterflies about the house, again to Mother's great delight and relief. She was now able to feast her eyes on a predatory beast, an Amur leopard no less, a sturdy male, which Edmund stuffed, with the family as keen onlookers. To see a flat-packed hide brought back to life as a proud specimen of the Panthera pardus orientalis species, posing on a dried tree trunk, ready for action, bursting with life, with realistic glass eyes and a roaring mouth, what sculptor can accomplish such a thing? It had previously been common to stuff the animals with straw and moss and build stands out of wooden slats to hold them upright. These materials were later replaced by plasticine, which was far more stable and longer-lasting, Edmund was a pioneer in that regard. Mother was very proud of Edmund, prouder than she was of me, and I had shot the animal.

But one evening when we were sitting alone in the parlour, she confided to me that both Father's disposition and character changed when our collections arrived from Vladivostok. Upon receipt of a telegram – he had instructed the steamship company to send one as soon as the cargo arrived – he would run down to the harbour right away, have the chests transported home, almost aloft in triumph, and open them with the piety and expectation of a child unwrapping Christmas presents. It could take him days and weeks; he was very moved. And I interpreted this in the best way, even though Father never (or at least very rarely) made any mention of it to us, his sons. I think I understand why Mother told me this in private.

It took us nearly six months to distribute and sell the rich yield. And being still without any form of financial support, either of a private or public character, we were dependent upon this income.

After all, surely a new expedition beckoned?

Indeed it did: not many weeks had passed before we hardly spoke of anything else. We had drafted several alternatives, when in the late spring of 1896 I heard by chance that the price of Siberian deer antlers had grown sky-high in Europe, inspiring Henry and myself to embark on a hasty fundraising trip to Yablonovy in the Transbaikal, a summer trip. Edmund wanted to stay at home and continue his work as a taxidermist at Umlauffsches Museum, and furthermore had fallen in love, planned to marry, and claimed to be happier than a pig in mud.

68

We travelled overland, first by railway, as far as it would take us, then by horse. Owing to various stopovers along the way, we did not arrive at the foot of Yablonovy until June 18. However, we managed to collect a total of 5,000 butterflies and moths there.

But it was the deer antlers we were really after, and we had a stroke of good fortune in that regard: the Cossacks who had at one time put us up in Listvyanka told us about some Russian hunters who had been hunting deer further south in the mountains for years. They probably had piles of antlers lying around, so we would not even have to shoot the animals ourselves.

We departed by horse and wagon, on terrible roads – they say Siberia has no roads, only distances – and soon managed to track down the hunters in question. Within a few days we had negotiated the purchase of 1,030 pairs of antlers, many with interesting abnormalities, with, as it turned out, a resale value in Germany of 21,000 marks. An enormous sum at the time, guaranteeing us many new years in the wilderness.

We left Transbaikal by late August, travelling again by road. It took almost two months. We reached Achinsk on October 20. From there we could go by rail via Moscow to Warsaw. After a short stay in the Polish capital, we continued on, arriving in Hamburg with the precious antlers in early November. In the space of the six months, we had travelled more than twenty thousand miles, one of our shortest, fastest expeditions, and without doubt the most profitable.

69

The plan, as I said, was to finance a more extensive expedition and to get Henry's business up and running. And we were well under way with both when a watershed occurred in my life: during my previous visit home, I had met a girl, and after the short trip to Baikal we had met almost daily, until the point – which took me quite by surprise – where I had to acknowledge that she had become indispensable. I thought of little else, morning, noon and night. Now the question appeared to be whether it would be love rather than age that tore me away from the wilderness.

The object of my affection was a true *Hamburgerin*, twenty-three years my junior, indescribably beautiful, intelligent and kind, but rather headstrong, something I viewed as a sign of character. Her name was Alina Lerche, her surname being the German for "lark", which I took for a good omen. In the course of spring – I must repeat that we saw each other every day – I ventured to ask for her hand and she formally accepted, so we were engaged in late spring and married on August 14, 1897.

Under her spell, within just six months, I had become as accustomed to civilisation again as my little brother Edmund. The antler venture had left me fairly well-to-do, and if one added in the income from the

5,000 butterflies we had collected on the same trip, one was left with the picture of a man in his prime.

Henry, naturally, did not like this turn of events one bit. He remained the only brother never to marry. He continued working away on his business, which he had decided to establish in Stellingen, but was also negotiating the purchase of a house in Vladivostok. (He would in time apply for Russian citizenship, and have it granted, with the signature of the tsar himself on the ornate papers.)

Our honeymoon did not pass completely as planned however, quite the contrary in fact. We were travelling by horse and cart one hot summer day towards Blankenese, north of Hamburg, happily minding our own business, when I spotted Carl Hagenbeck, my old source of inspiration, standing by the side of the road waving a handkerchief, looking lost. Naturally I stopped and asked if he needed help. No, no, in fact I was the one he was looking for.

I introduced him to my young wife. He praised her in profuse terms, before quickly turning to the heart of the matter:

"Such good fortune to have encountered you both. Congratulations on your marriage, when did the nuptials take place?"

"A month ago."

That was quite long enough, in his opinion, and furthermore, one can take a honeymoon at any time at all. What he needed me to do now was return to Siberia, capture twenty specimens of Dybowski's sika deer and transport them back to Europe alive for sale to the Duke of Bedford in England.

I knew well who Bedford was. He ran a famous zoological garden at Woburn Abbey, a modern park, where the animals were uncaged and free to roam in the extensive grounds, an idea Hagenbeck was also hoping to realise in Hamburg. He told me the duke would pay a very high price for these animals, which were entirely unfamiliar to Europeans.

"You can manage it in ten months."

I have to say I was flabbergasted. The Dybowski's had, in a manner of speaking, been my deer, I had killed and prepared quite a few of them, so Hagenbeck knew what he was doing when he singled me out to take on the task.

Alina could not believe her ears, she had by this stage gathered an idea of the kind of life we lived in the field. The situation resembled one we were all too familiar with in our family, namely the story of our father arriving late to his wedding because he had been detained by some birds along the way, and when he did finally show up at the church, the pockets of his morning suit were stuffed with live sparrows.

But the short conversation with Hagenbeck struck a chord deep down inside – just one more trip! And moreover: live animals, not pre-pared furs. It was both a challenge and a chance to ease the sense of unfinished business I had felt ever since I had captured Yascha the tiger and sold him to the circus.

Negotiations proved tense and feelings ran high, but eventually Aline gave me permission to travel, when I vowed that it would be my very last trip, and that I would come home safe and sound. I gave her my solemn word on both counts, unaware that it would turn out to be my most complicated and perilous expedition, due in no small part to how badly planned it was, something I myself must take responsibility for.

70

For bureaucratic reasons, I had to stop by the Zoological Museum in Moscow again to obtain the necessary papers, so I took an overland route; this would turn out to be my first mistake, as it was already too late in the year.

Carl Hagenbeck and his son Heinrich accompanied me to Moscow, where they had some business to attend to. I had known Carl since childhood, when I was sent to the Hagenbeck family's pet shop as a six-year-old boy to buy feed for Father's birds. Carl was twelve or thirteen back then, a considerable age gap when one is so young, but we shared an interest in animals and soon struck out on expeditions together, capturing frogs, snails, birds and insects . . . On one occasion I forgot the time, and the curfew, and returned too late at the city gate and had to pay a fine of eight pfennig to *Die Wache des Bürgermilitärs*, I remember it as though it happened yesterday.

By October 9 all the formalities were in place and the Hagenbecks followed me to the railway station, both in bear furs and puffing on cigars. I travelled by rail east towards Omsk, alone, keenly feeling Henry's absence. He was on a short expedition north to Scandinavia, also commissioned by Hagenbeck.

At Omsk I alighted from the train and continued my journey aboard a river steamer on the Irtysh. But we had got no further than Pavlodar when we encountered so much drift ice that the rest of the voyage was cancelled, in fact all shipping ceased for the winter, and I was not even halfway between Omsk and the Altay Mountains, my first destination on this leg.

Nevertheless, I decided to press onwards. This was my second mistake.

I travelled the four hundred kilometres to Semipalatinsk by horse and sleigh, along with a hired *yamshchik*, as Russians call their drivers, a dogged, indomitable chap who knew the region well.

The journey took us across many miles of steppes, not a single tree to be seen, only stalks of dry grass waving above the snow-covered ground, and unceasing wind. Fine-grained snow whipped at our eyes constantly and carpeted the terrain so thickly that the horses barely got purchase with their hooves.

After a long day in terrible weather, we arrived at a post station with no room for us inside. As it was impossible to travel further, we unhitched the horses, tethered them behind the sleigh and gave them hay. A patient Kyrgyz horse feels at home where it is fed. Incidentally, my *yamshchik* was also Kyrgyz, and every time we changed horses, he always asked if there were any Kyrgyz horses available. When I inquired as to why, he told me he liked to speak in his mother tongue to the animals.

We huddled down in the sleigh, enjoying the black bread I always carry with me, pulled the fur over our heads, and let the wind and weather race across the earth. It was a long night and the next morning the conditions were just as impossible.

It was midday before the storm had abated sufficiently to allow us to continue, but only at a careful pace. On our way we passed a broken-down sleigh with three dead horses still harnessed but no sign of any people. We arrived at the next station late at night, and fortunately there was room for us indoors.

We progressed in this way, stage by stage, in that unfathomable land-scape, until we finally reached Semipalatinsk on the banks of the Irtysh, where in 1718 the Russians had established a fort on the ruins of an old Buddhist monastery. Over the years a small town had grown up around the fort, a crossroads and trading post in the land of the nomads.

I spent five days roaming the area to obtain an overview of the wild animal population, wrote a detailed report to Hagenbeck, and sent it with the westbound post before we continued on. This survey was one of the reasons I had chosen to travel overland.

Along the way, Alina and the Dybowski's deer to be captured on the Siberian coast were foremost in my thoughts, so to get a head start on winter we drove day and night. Our route took us over Barnaul, by the upper reaches of the River Ob, one of the largest and wealthiest towns in Siberia, thanks to the enormous silver deposits in Altay. From there we went on towards Biysk, and about halfway there a fuzzy grey shadow turned up in the snowstorm ahead of us.

It turned out to be a sleigh. As we drew closer, we could see the horses were being attacked by a pack of wolves. At my behest, the *yamshchik* increased our speed and within a few minutes we were at the centre of the drama. The wolves soon gave up and fled but I managed to place a bullet in one, causing it to limp, and killed it with my next shot.

The driver of the sleigh, hearing the shots, appeared shortly afterwards.

He had walked a few hundred metres further on to check if the ice on the river would hold. His poor horses had put up a brave fight but had had some terrible bites inflicted upon them which were difficult to bandage in the cold, although we did our best.

We travelled on together and, following much limping and exertion, we got both sleighs to Biysk.

We bade farewell to our new friend and continued undaunted via Krasnoyarsk to Irkutsk, a distance of about 2,200 kilometres, which took us almost three weeks. But my memories of this part of the journey range from the very vague to next to nothing. Today, thinking back, the entire stretch seems like a grey series of hazy circumstances characterised by repetition. I can only assume we got into a rhythm that rendered both the days and nights indistinguishable from one another. According to the psychologist Sigmund Freud, there is a reason one remembers what one remembers and likewise forgets what one forgets, and it is not only tied up with the nature of experience but with one's personality. When I first read this, I thought it seemed far-fetched, but now I am inclined to believe he was on to something. It was one of the hardest journeys I have been on, so no doubt I ensconced myself in some personal armour of sorts, and when I finally emerged, it crumbled like the pupa of a butterfly.

In Irkutsk we changed horses, leaving immediately for Baikal, where we had to continue south of the lake as the surface had yet to freeze over. Fortunately, there lay sufficient snow in the mountains, so we travelled on to the town of Kyakhta, meaning we had journeyed a further 700 kilometres over the past ten days, and I decided we would stop for the day there to rest.

71

The journey from Kyakhta along the Mongolian border at the foot of the Yablonovy Mountains was covered in the same open sleigh in temperatures of thirty-two degrees below zero. But being well clothed, we did not find it unpleasant, even in the quivering frost. To the south we had a gently undulating landscape, the endless Mongolian plains, covered in snow, or a mantle of ice rather, and to the north a sparse forest of pine.

When we arrived at Yablonovy I paid the *yamshchik*. We parted without saying much more to each other than "thank you"; I thanked him for his perseverance, and he thanked me for the money, and I can still recall his face, but not his name, and that strikes me as curious. I asked him what he intended to do, and he told me he would seek lodgings nearby and wait.

"Wait for what?" I enquired.

He did not know; for spring, I suppose.

I went on several miles alone to the farm of a Cossack I was acquainted with, a small, wiry and likeable fellow my own age who lived with his elderly parents in a house he had built himself. His name was Andrey

Simukhin, and during the summer he was employed by the postal service, while in the winter he hunted, also specialising in fishing with a net beneath the river ice.

I wanted to purchase two Russian horses from Andrey and journey onwards alone. But he offered to accompany me, as the postal route ended where he resided. He could then bring the horses back and I would avoid the cost of hiring them.

I thanked him for his kindness, and after a couple of days' rest, the horses were hitched up. To keep ourselves warm in the severe cold we had to wade through the deep snow alongside the sleigh for the first few days. This winter was by all accounts particularly harsh. When we stopped for the night on the fourth day, at an altitude of 4,500 feet, we measured the temperature at forty-three below zero. We chopped bread into pieces with an axe and soaked it in melted snow, just to grind crunchy icy slush between our molars. The campfire did not give off enough heat, so sleep was out of the question.

The evening sky illuminated the snow-covered mountaintops while the crimson glow over the horizon in the west warned of more polar cold. In the light from the fire, we saw an old wolf on his last hunt, scratching about the snow-bare mountainsides in a futile attempt to quell the clamorous hunger in his belly. He lay in wait where I had observed the tracks of some argali earlier, probably looking for lichen and dried herbs. The stars rose higher, semi-darkness spread over the silent hills, the naked trees cast dead shadows across the snow, and since we could not sleep I decided to take a wander in the magical night and flushed out a black grouse (*Tetrao tetrix*) that had dug itself down to seek shelter from the frost. It was the only sign of life I saw, apart from the dying wolf, which incidentally I put down before we moved on.

At noon the following day a dark figure with arms flailing wildly suddenly appeared in front of the horses. It turned out to be a Russian soldier, a large, sturdy fellow in his early twenties. But he was weeping like a child, raving and begging us for food; he was snow-blind into the bargain. We laid him down in the sleigh, bundling him up in what blankets and furs we had, and through teeth chattering with cold, he told us he had set out with twenty men a fortnight earlier to take altitude measurements. All his comrades, including the commanding officer, had died from starvation or cold, and he was the sole survivor.

We brought the half-dead man with us.

When we reached the highest pass in Yablonovy, at a height of 5,600 feet, a wonderful panorama of immense mountains opened before us, shrouded in light mist, with countless valleys between the ridges, each disappearing in bottomless depths. An eagle soared above us, sailing majestically over the extraordinary land below. Man's insignificance, and especially my own smallness, has never seemed clearer to me.

To the south we could make out the Buryat witch mountain, Sochonda, rising up to almost 7,000 feet, and to the north a series of small white points over the pink shroud of frost. At the most strenuous descent we had to lead the horses by their bridles, though they constantly stumbled and fell all the same. We had to stop and rest continually and used a lot of time getting water from ice-covered streams we had to hack at. But after three days Yablonovy was behind us, and we were alive.

In a village by the River Ingoda we left our soldier friend at the house of some Russian civilians who promised to look after him for a small sum. He was lucid, no longer blind, and would likely survive.

I said my goodbyes to Simukhin here also. And it was no easy parting. He shook my hand and said, "I'll never see you again".

Along with the Kyrgyz *yamshchik*, he was the man I had learned to place the most trust in of all those I had travelled with, besides my brothers, so I clasped his hand and made no reply.

I hired three horses and continued alone, following the Onon south, first along the bank because the river was only partially frozen. Then uphill along the Mongolian border until I reached the Abagatui frontier post, which Simukhin had marked on my map. It was manned by Cossacks. I allowed myself a few days rest with these friendly souls in north-eastern Mongolia, whilst also surveying the mammal population in the area, yet another of Hagenbeck's assignments, and the third – or was it the fourth? – reason for my choosing to travel overland. But my stay here would prove longer than planned.

72

Winter is a time of peace and quiet in that cold and temperate zone, when one truly feels the emptiness of the world in mind and body, something everyone should expose themselves to, not least to learn to appreciate life. The first time I made my way onto the steppes around Abagatui the feeling was overwhelming, I have no words for that winter, and had I known then that I would survive, I would have been happy to acknowledge something so profound, but at the time I did not know what to think, I was probably filled with a kind of awe.

The horizon was infinite, some grey snow clouds in the north-west, air so pure and crystal clear that one's gaze never rested. Some snow buntings fluttered around at a loss in the settlement looking for seeds on the ragged glasswort: in the summer and autumn months these plants cover the landscape in an explosion of iridescent colour. A pair of ravens, resident in the settlement, stayed indoors. The streets were deserted. The windows of the log houses were small and shuttered. Dogs sought refuge in the innermost parts of the houses, and hens curled up into balls together beneath ovens, probably with plans to hibernate. And now new snow clouds piled up in the sky.

But the Mongols and Buryats knew no fear.

They had lived with these inhospitable conditions from birth. Dressed in long-armed, wide sheepskin coats, they mounted their indispensable horses every day. They knew the steppe and the sky above it, knew every stone, every hill and water source, and had given names to every rock formation to be found. They could predict the weather with great accuracy and knew exactly what they had to do to protect people and livestock.

Nevertheless, now they grew uneasy – something was brewing.

In the space of what seemed like seconds, the wind whipped the snow so hard in between the dwellings that they stood as one with the terrain around, the steppes became a land of death and doom. The gusts threatened to overturn the cloth yurts and tore the roof off two houses, sending people and animals running around in a daze. A pale disk of sun was still just discernible through the blowing snow, until it flickered out, turning everything into flitting shadows through the vision of a half-blind man. The cold became even more unbearable, the crystals cutting at our faces, we could not see, could not be outside, but had to be, for a storm like this could last up to thirty-six hours and the livestock could not survive that.

The animals had to brought home – but *against* the wind. And only the strongest managed, whilst one animal after another succumbed to the elements and vanished like headless chickens in white smoke, perhaps in the final hope of dropping down into a depression or a small crevice. Or of rushing over a precipice. Or of perishing on the muddy banks of the salt lake, which never froze.

The same happened with the precious horses: the weakest galloped in front of the storm, tails raised, manes fluttering, disappearing one after another. At the closest station to the west, a total of ten animals had been lost in a similar storm the previous winter.

We saved those that could be saved. And in the early evening of that terrible day something even stranger happened: the storm began to go through noticeable, very sudden phases, like the steps of a staircase, the howls grew weaker and fewer, the disk of sun became discernible in small flashes, the house ravens took flight, the snow buntings peeped out from the eaves and the Mongols could breathe a collective sigh of relief and crawl into bed in their yurts – but what had become of the snow?

There was hardly any left on the surrounding steppes. The plains were bare and black as a desert of coal, only painted here and there with white brushstrokes, any slight unevenness in the terrain now packed with snow, like the coat of a zebra, like nothing I had ever seen, and the stripes shifted from hour to hour.

73

In my report to Hagenbeck I wrote (amongst other things): In addition to wolves, the corsac fox (*Vulpes corsac*) also hunts in this region, a nocturnal species which keeps to the marmots' abandoned burrows, catching water voles, and constantly falls victim to the Mongols' self-triggered arrows, as its pelage is much prized.

A herd of gazelles (*Antilope gutterosa*) had come to the area to graze on last year's undergrowth along the riverbanks. But it was not possible to get within shooting range of them on the open steppe. Usually, they are driven towards the hunters in battue-like fashion. But even the most experienced beaters now had problems getting the animals to stand still, especially on the snow-bare plains, as they were particularly jumpy and shy owing to a shortage of water.

On the Daurian steppe on the Russian side, the gazelles gather in two areas in particular, calving when the Lilium tenuifolium bloom in June, at one spot east of Lake Dsun-Tarei, and another south of Soktui. And although these beautiful animals usually migrate from Mongolia to Russia in early winter, it has been a long time since they were observed here west of Tarei. I have been informed that their presence varies from winter to winter. According to the local hunters, two things in particular define the gazelles' migratory pattern: the herbaceous plant growth in the Gobi Desert and the first snowfall. If winter comes late, the animals can arrive in October or November, and will then wander over the Blue Mountains, as far as the River Ononborsa.

The Cossacks I lived with told me that the wild donkeys, or onagers (*equus heminus*), move in between the border posts at Soktui and Abagatui in the autumn. Widespread migration begins when last year's foals can keep up with the mares, each herd under the leadership of an old stallion. At the close of September, the young stallions leave the groups they have belonged to for three years, to roam more mountainous terrain individually, in order to form new herds.

During migration the onager is at its most obstreperous, calling to mind certain words about Ishmael: "He shall be a wild donkey of a man . . ."

The young stallion can stand for hours facing the wind, nostrils wide open, scanning the landscape. Filled with pugnacity, waiting for a potential adversary, whom it will suddenly lurch in the direction of to initiate a bloody struggle for the favour of the mares. With tail raised and mane bristling, it will race past the leader of the herd, kicking at him with its hind legs as it passes. After some further jumps he will stop, turn to the side and circle the flock in a large arc, his covetous gaze always fixed on the leader, the old, vigilant stallion, who has no other choice but to wait patiently for the challenger to draw close enough; only then can he attempt to attack, biting and kicking to the best of his ability.

The Mongols take advantage of these fights to hunt the younger stallions, whose meat is delicious, as I can personally attest. Furthermore, their hide fetches a good price. On such hunts, the Mongols will leave very early in the day – always taking a pale-yellow horse along and usually riding into the mountains south-west of Soktui, moving slowly through the wilderness while scouring the area with hawk-eyed scrutiny. As soon as the hunters catch sight of a black dot on the horizon, they urge their horses to a gallop, careful to keep to the hollows and dips in the terrain and always riding into the wind.

Then the real hunt begins.

The pale-yellow horse has its tail hairs bound together and, with saddle removed, it is led to a height, where it wanders freely grazing, while the hunter lies down to wait with rifle resting on a short fork. After a while the onagers spot the horse and, believing it to be a mare of their species, will gallop closer, before sooner or later discovering their error and wavering. This hesitation is the hunter's moment, the only chance he will get. Struck in the shoulder by a precise shot, the young stallion will throw itself around, making a few desperate leaps, before falling over.

Several years ago, there were also wild sheep here, argali (*Ovis ammon*). They can grow to be very large, more than one hundred and fifty centimetres from ground to shoulder, and the horns of the ram can measure up to one hundred and twenty centimetres and weigh up to twenty kilos. These animals are much sought after and fetch a high price. Here in the border areas of Mongolia, one finds them nowadays usually nine hundred kilometres further south, on the so-called highland steppe.

74

After staying just more than a week with the Mongols in Abagatui, I got back onto the sleigh, together with a new *yamshchik*, a Russian of slight appearance who had sought refuge there due to the weather. It was 2,500 kilometres to my destination. And we would meet our fair share of obstacles along the way.

Even prior to reaching Pokrovka, a Cossack village by the Amur, our problems began. Dense drifting ice flowed in all the rivers and streams, often pressing together and piling up into metre-high packs which we had to chop through with an axe. It could take one or two hours to traverse even the narrowest watercourse, and the horses were often soaked and needed to rest and get dry, preferably by a campfire.

Fortunately, the post stations were located no further than twenty-five or thirty versts apart, so between battling the elements we could warm ourselves up and hire new animals.

We passed steep, pine-covered mountains in grotesque formations, negotiated deep corries, and went over naked plains, through one type of snowy weather after another.

Some insects, oddly enough, fared extremely well in the terrible conditions, and as I had of course my collector's equipment along with me, I made several interesting discoveries along the way. But for the deer it was a merciless time; we encountered many specimens who had succumbed.

On the twelfth day, along the Amur, our sleigh lost a runner, but we found a village shortly afterwards, where miraculously a blacksmith lived, and he helped us repair the damage. And as the moon again rose over the landscape, we harnessed the horses and went on.

A new thirty-verst stage of our journey lay ahead of us.

The snow had been blown off the ground along certain stretches, so we had to walk alongside the sleigh, letting the horses pull it over exposed rocky outcrops, necessitating constant stops for repairs and rest. After a while I suggested to the *yamshchik* that we try our luck on the Amur, surely here the ice would hold?

It did, and the going proved much easier. In temperatures of thirty-four below zero with bright moonlight, the horses – which we shod with spikes – could really hit their stride downriver. I asked the *yam-shchik* if he had been this way before and he said he had not. I told him how six or seven years previously my brothers and I had sailed leisurely downstream with the current in glorious late summer weather, quite a surreal memory, because one simply had to accept if one's only experience of the Amur was in summertime, one had not the foggiest idea of its true nature.

The Amur rises where the Shilka and the Argu meet, the former flowing from Russia, the latter from China. From this confluence, the Amur behaves like a capricious youth, alternating between cascading rapids and deep, slow-flowing stretches, continuously fuelled by plentiful tributaries, until after two thousand kilometres it spreads out like a sea flowing through the land, before finally becoming lost in the huge delta by the Sea of Okhotsk. The Amur is one of the most important rivers on the planet, in terms of its intricate character, its abundance and beauty, and not least due to its significance as a natural border between the mighty empires of Russia and China.

75

One night, while following one of the many branches of the river, we missed a station obscured behind an island. All we could do was continue to the next station on empty stomachs. But when the sky eventually began to brighten in the east there was no village nor station to be seen. I then began to experience shivering in my body, a sign of blood flowing to the heart. I was filled with an unfamiliar but extremely pleasant warmth. I was, in short, on the verge of passing out.

But a sudden jolt to the sleigh roused me. When I opened my eyes, everything around was quiet and peaceful. I noticed I had begun to grow cold again, a sign that the blood was circulating in my veins anew and that life was returning.

The exhausted horses were standing perfectly still beside the sleigh, close to one another to keep warm. But the *yamshchik* was nowhere to be seen. I hopped out and found him lying between the legs of the horses. It was his fall I could thank for bringing me round and thus for keeping me alive, and just in the nick of time; another few minutes and both we and the horses would have been food for the wolves.

I tried to resuscitate the poor wretch by rubbing him vigorously and rolling him back and forth on the ice. It took twenty minutes to bring him round. To keep death at bay we jogged alongside the sleigh for approximately fifteen versts, until fortunately we found a station not marked on the map.

The *yamshchik*'s feet, nose and ears were badly frostbitten, as were his hands. I had damage to my feet and face, but had otherwise got off with just a scare. We were fed, warmed ourselves up, and slept for a few hours. But the *yamshchik* was in no state to carry on. My feet, meanwhile, had recovered: running the last versts had no doubt helped.

We bade farewell to one another. I have warm memories of him, and this parting was not an easy one either. Fortunately, neither he nor I said anything as I paid him and we shook hands.

I continued alone. On the ice again at first, for ten days, as far as Khabarovsk, a town springing up out of nowhere in the wilderness. But I only stopped to change horses, making my way further up the mighty Ussuri, where the stations lay as close as on the Amur. Then I pressed on in a dreadful crosswind over Lake Khanka, which took me three whole days to cross, without sleep. And on February 22 I arrived quite famished and frozen in dear old Vladivostok, where I could lodge with Hans Gammenthaler, who greeted me in his customary fashion whenever I turned up in this manner.

That same evening, sitting under the old tiger skull, with a glass of cognac and a pipe, I added up the distances covered, first from Pavlodar to Altay, and then to here on the east coast via Yablonovy, with all the detours, and worked out that the little sleigh had carried me a total of 5,990 kilometres (in actual fact 9,923 kilometres on later calculation).

76

In Vladivostok there was little time for contemplation – after all, I had promised Hagenbeck I would return with the deer within ten months. Not to mention the promises I had made to Alina. The last letter I had sent to her was from Semipalatinsk, but God knows if it had arrived, in any case there were no letters waiting for me in Vladivostok, only two telegrams: one from an impatient Hagenbeck and one from Father, looking for signs of life, but he sent greetings from the family at least, and from Alina.

The cold on the east coast of Siberia is not as insufferable as inland, the temperatures at this time of year lie between twelve and eighteen below zero, which is pleasant when one is accustomed to harsher conditions.

Together with a hunter I was acquainted with, Ivan Kamsky, who I knew was good with deer, I rode through the Suchan Valley, arriving three days later at the foot of the Sjantalase Mountains, where previously I had recorded the largest population of Dybowski's deer as well as captured the eagles. And we soon found tracks – a trail in fact, that the animals had made encircling the eternal tooth-like mountain – that looked very promising, and by then I had hatched a plan on how proceed.

Ivan took it upon himself to set up a temporary camp while I rode to Chimochhae to have large boxes made to transport the animals. In order to ensure my instructions were carried out precisely I had to remain in the village while the work took place. Then, unfortunately, I had to return to Vladivostok due to my lack of prescience, and purchase wire fencing for an enclosure, as well as hire six Russian workers to build it.

On our way back through the mountains we were surprised by a snowstorm lasting two days. But eventually we made it to Sjantalase, where we immediately set to work constructing the enclosures, which took four days.

We built the pens in loops to prevent the animals from finding a way out once they had first entered. At the centre, narrow stalls were put in place so they would be stuck. All we had to do was lure them in with food, of which there was little in the woods at this time of year, but at least that was something I had prepared for.

Naturally, our racket had disturbed the deer, so there was little hope of capturing any of them over the next few days. A short distance away I shot two roe deer, which we made a hearty soup from. And this is also a good memory, so many men engaged in a common purpose sitting around a fire eating a good meal – in addition, I could conclude that I had hired both hardy and reliable people.

Just enough snow fell on the third night to cover our tracks. I clambered up onto a ridge behind the bivouac in the morning and, through field glasses, could see that two deer had trapped themselves in the enclosure. But we could not approach them without giving away our presence.

On the seventh day a further five deer became trapped in the pen, four older bucks and a young hind. We approached cautiously and drove the animals into the centre of the enclosure. It was not hard to imagine their mortal fear, the thudding and pounding of their hearts as eight rough pairs of human hands lifted them up one by one and shoved them into a wooden box on their own. And again, I could observe the curious sight of several of the animals playing possum when faced with danger, keeling over and lying stiff as corpses in the snow, that is of course if they had not fainted from shock. The workers were convinced we had killed them. But then they simply stood up again, alive and kicking, and the extensive taming and tending could begin.

We ensured they had an abundance of oak branches, poplar twigs, black bread and aromatic hay, as well as enough fresh water. Four days later both the bucks and the young hinds had adapted to captivity. But they would only countenance being fed and watered by a single person, a task I undertook with pleasure.

Four days later another snowfall covered up all the old tracks. The next morning, climbing atop our lookout post, I was close to howling with joy. I crept back down and informed the others: a further three bucks, six fully-grown hinds and five of the previous year's fawns had entered the enclosure. One hind and three fawns had managed to break free before we made it down, but still, we now had a total of fifteen animals.

We settled down again to mark time until it snowed.

But on this occasion our wait was in vain, and life in the bivouac was getting unpleasant, the temperature remained between ten and twenty below zero the whole time. We held out a further five days before I called off the operation and sent the men down to the nearest village to fetch horses and more sleighs. That took three days.

Despite our having to transport the large, cumbersome boxes along almost impassable mountain paths, while feeding and tending to the terrified animals at the same time, we reached Vladivostok in just eight days. I left two of the workers there to take care of the animals so Ivan and I could concentrate on getting hold of the five specimens outstanding.

77

We rode to a stunning mountainous region north-west of the town, where we had heard some Old Believers kept Dybowskis on account of their antlers. A two-metre-high plank fence surrounded the residence, and the gate was closed when we arrived, so I pulled the bell cord. Eventually, we heard a frail female voice through a small opening asking what we wanted. I replied that we wished to stay the night, adding that we would also like to speak with the owner.

She slammed the peephole shut and disappeared. It was several minutes before we heard another voice through the gate, a man's this time, enquiring as to whether we had dogs with us. I said no, and he opened, took our horses and led us to a house where we were shown up to the first floor. There were two long benches with straw and some woven bedspreads in the room, and agreeable heat emanating from a large stove. A worker brought us a jug of hot water and asked if we smoked tobacco. We told him we did, and he left the room coughing expressions of displeasure.

While we sat eating, I noticed some faint movement in the curtain above the stove. It was not being caused by the heat, so I nudged my friend and said:

"We're not alone here, Ivan, look above the stove."

The curtain moved again. I jumped up and pulled it aside and found myself staring into the face of a shrivelled, skeletal, ancient-looking woman, and neither before nor since have I ever seen someone so desiccated yet still alive.

I later learned that the mummy-like woman was one hundred and nineteen years old and the mother of the deer farmer, who himself was in his nineties. The Old Believers treat these women as sacred, to be worshipped and treated in the manner appropriate, and provided with all they require of food and drink. But they have to lie in dark prisons like this one, where not a ray of light can penetrate, waiting for death to liberate them.

We made ourselves as comfortable as we could on the benches, and the night passed in silence, apart from a slight, recurring throat-clearing from the compartment above the stove. Next morning, we had just dressed ourselves when the door opened and an old, white-bearded man entered and sat down at a bench at the window. Several minutes went by without his saying a word. I did not take my eyes from him, but he remained silent.

As we had hoped to return that same evening with the animals we lacked, I grew slightly dejected, and got up, went over to stand in front of him and said, in a loud voice, in case he was deaf:

"I've come to buy five deer."

He also got to his feet, and proclaimed:

"I'm willing to show you around the farm but none of my animals are for sale."

This was too much, so I reached into my bag and took out the document I had been issued by the director of the Zoological Museum in Moscow, stating that every Russian keeping deer in Siberia was obliged to sell me the animals I might require.

The old man could not read, but recognised the seal of the tsar and instantly grew more amenable. Thus, I was able to select five beautiful young specimens, paying him two hundred roubles as a first instalment.

While the horses were being saddled, we were in the kitchen making conversation when I noticed a barrel of water, unclipped my cup from my belt, and filled it up. On seeing this, the old man called out to two labourers who immediately came and pushed over the barrel, flooding the kitchen, supposedly because I had contaminated the water.

Once we had mounted our horses, I thought it fitting to share some cognac to celebrate our deal. I took a gulp, handed the hipflask to Ivan, who took a sip, and then passed it to the old man. It was just as contaminated as the water, as our lips had come into contact with it, but that did not prevent him from knocking back almost the entire contents. I leaned towards my friend and whispered:

"If that's how it is, Ivan, I'd rather not believe at all than halfway."

We rode to the nearest village, where Ivan stayed on to supervise the construction of five new animal boxes, after which he would see to the transportation of the deer, while I continued to Vladivostok and lodged with Gammenthaler as usual. A week later, Ivan arrived with the shipment. I had my twenty animals.

However, I had to wait almost a fortnight for the Japanese steamer *Tairon Maru* to take me and my cargo to Japan. In the meantime, I ran into my old friend Hoeck. He had grown considerably older in the past few years and told me he was in the process of selling his schooner and had found an interested buyer, though he thought the offer too low. He was now willing to wait until the summer and had also put his residence on Sidimi on the market, in order to travel home to Holland to enjoy his golden years in his childhood district of Scheveningen, which he had not seen since he left aged twelve, forty-five years previously. I told him Henry was planning to buy a house in Vladivostok and settle down here.

"He's young," Hoeck replied drily.

We spent a few pleasant days together at Gammenthaler's. And when the *Tairon Maru* finally docked, and we had loaded aboard the animal boxes and feed I had bought, both men stood on the quay to say farewell. I gave Hoeck my family's address and our parting words were, "See you in Hamburg." Gammenthaler said, "You're welcome back."

After several tedious stopovers in Hokkaido, Yokohama and Osaka, we eventually reached Kobe, where it turned out I again faced a wait, of almost two weeks this time, for the German steamship *Niobe*. The animal boxes were unloaded, and the harbour master granted me permission to house them in a fish hall currently standing empty. I also managed to get in touch with people who could deliver the additional feed all these delays necessitated, no easy task in a country with hardly any cattle or sheep to speak of. And word of my curious cargo spread quickly through the town. In the afternoons, people came from far and wide to admire the beautiful creatures, and I felt like the attendant at a zoo, setting up cordons so they would not scare the animals, and could almost certainly have earned a tidy sum if I had sold tickets.

A lot had happened in the twenty years since I was last there. The owner of the ryokan I boarded at was both friendly and obliging, he even spoke a little French. The harbour resembled any other international port; many languages could be heard in the streets, and the presence of a European no longer caused a stir.

The *Niobe* finally docked. We loaded the animals aboard using modern cranes, stacking and securing the boxes on deck so I could walk between them to maintain close contact with every single animal. I stretched out two awnings of white canvas to form a canopy above them, and had brought my own water tanks – at Hagenbeck's insistence. He was obsessed with the welfare of the animals, and had been ever since one of his collectors, a Herr Menge, had been caught unawares by a hurricane several years ago while sailing around the Horn of Africa in a small steamship with forty-five live ostriches, a dozen beautiful beisa antelope, an equal number of gazelles and some other rare species. The animals either suffered terrible injuries from the merciless buffeting or were swept out to sea, and only six ostriches and three antelopes survived.

On May 20 we could eventually cast off and set sail for *die Heimat*!

78

We met no hurricanes on our voyage, not so much as a gale, and though the heat proved merciless at times, I had enough water to cool down the animals when the weather was at its hottest. Owing to unloading, bunkering of coal, and a lengthy quarantine we did not arrive in Hamburg until three months later, on August 8 to be exact. But we only stopped to bring Hagenbeck aboard, whom I had telegraphed ahead from Aden, and who had in the meantime prepared every detail regarding the last leg of our voyage to England.

We sailed directly to Dover with the deer – I did not even pop home – and took the train to Bedfordshire, where after an examination to declare them hale and hearty, the animals were let loose in Bedford's deer park at Woburn Abbey. And Hagenbeck was right, the Duke was beside himself with delight and paid much more than I had asked for. We ate an excellent dinner, took the return train to Dover at dawn the next day, and crossed on a passenger ship to Vlissingen in Holland. We then boarded another train, arriving in Hamburg on August 25.

(The herd had, incidentally, increased by two fawns en route, which came into the world in the Indian Ocean, with me acting as midwife.)

*

Alina met me on the steps of the house – after almost a year – overjoyed to have her old sea dog return, and in one piece. She had not received the letter from Semipalatinsk nor any telegram from Vladivostok and was convinced she would never see me again. I emphasised yet again that I had been exploring areas with poor communications, an explanation she found plausible but not particularly reassuring. But we were soon reconciled.

I now spent a lot of time at home, occupied with writing up reports on my latest trip, but also making efforts to find myself some employ in Hamburg; I wished to settle down in Altona, obey the clockwork of civilisation and spend my evenings in the company of Alina or listening to Father conversing with the many researchers and scientists who constantly called upon him. Seebom, Bolau and Hagenbeck, amongst others, were regular visitors.

But once again, the joys of domesticity were short-lived. In Central Asia, on the Vitim Plateau in Transbaikalia to be more precise, but also in Khentii and Yablonovy, plus by the sources of the Amur, there lived a wapiti deer which had two colours in winter. The head, neck and legs were a dark chestnut-brown, whilst the remainder of the body was silver-grey, with the exception of a yellow rump. Its antlers were also remarkable in every way, and this species had never been previously been brought back to Europe alive either.

So one day, Hagenbeck turned up and in customary fashion impressed upon me the need to bring back home five of these animals from Vitim, a trip that could now be done in just two months, in his opinion, since the Trans-Siberian Railway now extended all the way to Irkutsk. Neither did he fail to mention that I myself had described this species on my first journey to Baikal, when I visited the Bargusin Mountains with my brothers.

It was now September 1898, and I should be back in plenty of time for Christmas, Hagenbeck added optimistically, that is to say within the space of three months and not two, and I ought to have interpreted that as the bad sign it was.

But again I could not bring myself to say no, I was not yet quite finished with those icy wastes, and they were my deer, after all, the wapitis!

Once more there was uproar. Not only was Alina expecting – according to our physician we could anticipate delivery in late April or early May – but Henry had travelled by sea in order to settle down in Vladivostok, so I would have to journey alone again. All the same, Alina reluctantly allowed me to go, but only for the two months Hagenbeck had stipulated. She was no doubt comforted by the fact that the railway had not only made it more pleasant but also safer to travel. And I can bear witness to that.

79

On the train east from Moscow I both sat and slept like a lord in a comfortable and warm compartment in second class, surrounded by passengers in suits and frocks, in the care of a stern *provodnitsa* who tended and looked after us like a blacksmith and kept the samovar hot around the clock.

I made the entire journey from Hamburg to Irkutsk in just sixteen days, a marvel of a trip, like sitting at home in an armchair with a book while passing through tracts of land that had almost killed me the last time I covered them.

But things were soon to take a turn.

In Irkutsk I harboured a small hope of meeting the great expert on Siberia, Prince Kropotkin, geologist, geographer, zoologist and historian, as well as political rebel. I had read several studies he had written, all dealing with the self-same subjects that preoccupied me. The prince had also, as I mentioned previously, drawn up the maps we used. But unfortunately he was still in exile, in England or Switzerland presumably.

Happily, Hagenbeck had directed me to an affable old professor, who showed an immediate interest in the expedition and pointed out some locations in Vitim. He also put me in contact with people he considered reliable, hunters for the most part, Russians, all experienced.

I called upon them, one by one, evaluating them at leisure, and although it took some time, it meant I could avoid future disappointment. I bought in the equipment and the provisions I thought we needed for approximately two months, and we set out by horse and sleigh on the road to Baikal.

On the last section south along Lake Baikal I witnessed yet another of Siberia's many wonders. Over the course of the long autumn freeze, the storms had whipped the water from the lake up into the forests, coating the trees, cliffs and beaches in an inch-thick layer of ice, and then laying new layers upon them again, making it look as though bluish-white candle wax had rained over the land. As we travelled through this magical wonderland of glittering stalagmites, the phenomenon left my Russian companions just as spellbound as myself.

Upon reaching the Cossacks, the crucial question arose of whether the ice would hold. The last time I had been here with my Kyrgyz *yamshchik* we had had to go around the lake. They say Baikal holds the last drop of freshwater to freeze in Siberia, due to the tremendous volume of water to be cooled down. A Buryat once told me: "Baikal is as big and warm as your own heart." Before adding, with a serious expression, "When the water finally turns to ice, hope is lost." I am uncertain as to what he meant, but resolved now to interpret it in the best light, as if I had any choice.

According to the Cossacks, the lake had only iced over there in the south in the past few days, though still earlier than usual, and they had measured the temperature at fifteen to twenty below zero since then. They had also ventured out, but only on foot and close to land. Regarding conditions further north and by the mouths of the rivers, they had no knowledge.

Considering it would take at least a month to follow the shore around in challenging terrain, and perhaps two or three days to cross the lake on clear ice, the answer was self-evident. We discussed it amongst ourselves, then made a few holes, registering the thickness of the ice from six to thirteen centimetres, according to how close we were to the mouths of streams and rivers when we cut. The following morning all the holes were frozen over, plus a centimetre or two extra. I could not order anyone to undertake such a gamble, but none of the men wanted to back out. So after another three freezing cold days and nights, we packed what we needed onto the sleighs and set out across the clear, black ice, with our hearts in our mouths and a headwind from the north.

To the crunch of spiked hooves and hiss of runners we sat – careful to maintain a good distance between the sleighs – staring at the compass, counting the minutes and hours on our timepieces, glancing around us at the majestic snow-covered mountains floating in a pink, frosty mist over Asia, feeling smaller than when standing at the foot of the Yablonovy.

The ice on Lake Baikal has the unusual feature of freezing in stages, and being broken up again by wind between these stages, before freezing over completely again, resembling a patchwork of ice floes, stitched together in greyish-white seams, but also with crystal clear smooth surfaces, making it possible to see thirty or forty metres down into the deep. I experienced the feeling of sweeping over an uneven mosaic, and began to give serious thought to whether I would really be able to leave this life behind, whether I would ever manage to settle down with family and friends in a warm drawing room in Hamburg, because I had never felt more alive than I did at that moment.

But truth be told I was also settling an account of kinds, or formulating a will, a farewell. What one thinks will be eternal always turns out to be fleeting, a brief, quivering uncertainty, and then nothingness. For hour after hour it was not possible to tell by the landscape if we were in motion at all, the sound of the hooves and the runners, the decisive moment, it lasted for almost three days.

During that time we only rested once in a while and always at a safe distance from one another. We fed the jaded horses and gave them water from casks wrapped in fur, we did not dare cut at the ice, and there was no sleep for either man or beast.

Miraculously, we made it across in one piece, my Russian companions cheering in unison as we arrived at precisely the spot I had located on the map, south of the mouth of the Bargusin, where Henry, Edmund and I had arrived by boat on a hot summer's day almost a decade before. Now the landscape was unrecognisable.

We made it onto solid ground and let the exhausted animals rest for a couple of days.

Then we set out on the approximately 200 miles up through the Bargusin Valley, then via Vitim Valley towards the wildest mountainous region on the plateau, around one thousand metres above sea level. And it was an arduous trip.

We slept under the stars and many times had to take roundabout routes across the rugged landscape. And I was forced to acknowledge that the frostbite I had suffered in my leg two years previously had left a longer legacy than I assumed. The condition returned in the intense cold with renewed force, not as perceptible pain, but as a palsy, making it difficult for me to walk for long in deep snow. On the other hand, the conditions allowed me to take the true measure of the members of my party. Unfortunately, we had to shoot two horses along the way.

Since I did not have the time to capture these deer myself, I had to buy them, and that would prove to be quite expensive. Hagenbeck's contact in Irkutsk had informed me of some Tungus and Russians who kept deer in the region, on account of the antlers. And once we were up on the plateau we found the settlement before too long.

The bargaining went well, I got the wapitis I needed, wonderful creatures; these are large animals, the second biggest species of deer in the world, only surpassed by the elk. The males can weigh more than three hundred kilos, the females slightly less. I went from the muzzle of each animal to the next, speaking for a long time with each one, while they gazed anxiously back with clear, trusting eyes, as though posing questions to which there are no answers, the way animals have always looked at me really.

We led them into the wooden boxes we had built there in the space of three days, and placed one on each sleigh. And we bought four new horses.

Owing to an enormous snowfall our descent proved even more onerous than the ascent. It took us a total of eight hard days in thirty-two degrees below zero to manoeuvre the wooden boxes down to Lake Baikal. But on the morning of the ninth day we finally stood on the east bank. The lake lay stretching out before us in all its bright winter glory, blue ice in dazzling sunshine beneath sweeping, feather-light flour.

After our exertions in the mountains, the journey across the ice was child's play. Moreover, the feeling in my leg returned. And by the evening of the second day we reached the island of Olkhon, from where it was only 290 kilometres to the railway station in Irkutsk. But once again, we had problems in store.

80

Anyone who has travelled over Lake Baikal by horse and sleigh will have heard the fierce boom when the freezing water has set into metre-thick ice: the many small and large rivers flowing into the lake put surface ice under intense strain. Cracks, up to seven or eight hundred metres long, can open up with a resounding bang, the ice floes breaking and pressing up against each other to form small mountains, only to collapse into wet soup, creating impassable channels.

We now experienced this first hand.

Moving south along Olkhon, we managed only by unceasing effort to axe our way through the highest ice floes. When we found ourselves baulked by a four-metre wide open channel in the ice, with water cascading down. There was nothing for it but to wait until it collapsed back down.

An hour later it was a mere metre and a half across.

We laid down some planks, a necessity on such a crossing, so the horses could be led over one by one, whereupon we let them tow the sleighs and wooden boxes after them with a long rope.

Further out, more pack ice was constantly being forced up, and we could both hear the noise and feel the vibrations, but we thought the worst of it was behind us and picked up the pace again.

Then we caught sight of another sleigh, drawn by a team of three horses, travelling directly towards us at tremendous speed. As it drew closer we could see the driver standing in the sleigh, waving both arms and calling out at the top of his lungs. We could not make out a word he said but realised he must be terribly drunk, and when he was approximately one hundred metres from us he vanished from view.

We moved closer and found ourselves at the edge of a ten-metre wide open channel in the ice into which man, horses and sleigh had fallen. Only bubbles were visible beneath the black surface. Could we ourselves have vanished into this crack, if we had not witnessed the Russian reach it moments before us? Was he trying to warn us? Was he actually drunk? These are questions we will never get any answers to.

We skirted deftly around the channel, continuing south along Olkhon, making steady progress, until a strong wind suddenly came in from the north-west and began blowing over the large animal boxes. One of the hinds managed to scramble around, breaking a foreleg. Luckily she sustained no other injuries but I had to set the leg, which took time. After some more problems with the wind – which fortunately we eventually had at our backs – we again made landfall alive, again to much cheering in unison. I gave the men orders to break out the vodka, not a drop had passed our lips until that point.

Over the last fifty or sixty kilometres we had solid snow under the runners, and singing our way through the forests, we reached the railway station in Irkutsk on the afternoon of January 16, and could sleep indoors for the first time in more than four weeks. Personally, I checked into a hotel, but had to leave both windows open at night as it was too warm.

Three days later we loaded the animals aboard the train. As I generously paid some of the best men I have had in my employ, they looked at me as though thanking me for their being alive.

So I travelled west once more, in a warm carriage, through Russia's icy wastes, to Moscow, then on to Warsaw, with just a few minor bureaucratic interruptions along the way – quarantine was again an issue; crossing borders with live animals has never been a trifling matter, but I had the papers in order.

The deer shared a carriage with 110 bales of Chinese tea and were cosy given the circumstances. I nursed the hind with the broken leg and fed and watered them every time I myself had been to the dining car to put away a slap-up meal and a cognac.

These deer were also destined for the Duke of Bedford in England, and once again remuneration markedly exceeded the asking price. But parting with these animals proved more difficult than with my previous delivery; I was becoming more like Father in that regard, I suppose. How could I separate myself from these beautiful animals, whom I had tended to and fed for weeks, and who now obeyed me like trusting dogs? However, there was no doubt they would thrive at Woburn Abbey, the Duke loved animals as much as I did.

I was forced to leave in order to take care of the last leg of their journey, and was relieved of my anxieties a week later when a telegram came through from Woburn Abbey informing me that everything had passed without a hitch on the journey, the wapitis had arrived safe and sound and were settling in well. Four years later, I received a photograph of them from the Duke. All of them were still alive, had bred in addition, and now numbered fourteen.

Alina was in good health when I arrived home, her pregnancy well advanced judging by her stomach. She was very proud and made no fuss about the three extra months my trip had taken, perhaps due in no small part to the letters I had sent to reassure her, which she had received from Moscow, Omsk and Irkutsk, the last one – letter number two from Irkutsk – arriving a week after I had.

On May 7, 1899, our first daughter came into the world. We christened her Thecla, after one of Siberia's most beautiful butterflies. And the Lord God has since bestowed upon us many children and grandchildren, who still fill me with joy and inspiration.

After the journeys across the ice of Lake Baikal something had changed. For the first time in twenty-two years I was relieved to be alive, and to be home. Moreover, at forty-eight years of age, a sense of serenity had come over me. It also brought its own peace of mind knowing that in the course of the years we had captured and prepared approximately 61,000 Lepidoptera, whereof 275 were regarded as new species. In addition, there were approximately 42,000 beetles (Coleoptera), plus more than 5,550 birds (225 species), mammals and lesser species. I do not have an inventory of plants, but they were also of a significant number.

I worked more than a decade at the Museum of Ethnography in Hamburg, with responsibility for curating exhibitions and informing the public about the way of life of the many noble indigenous peoples in the east, primarily in Siberia. Subsequently, Hagenbeck charged me with constructing a dedicated *Insektenhaus* in Stellingen. I was more than happy to, and ran that with enthusiasm for twenty-four years.

Much is being written today about Siberia as an economic goldmine and a land of the future. Whilst I, in my ninetieth year, can sit in my study, lift my magnifying glass and once again admire an Apollo wide-eyed, study the fine lines and the delicate veins in the glassy wings, ever-changing in the invisible rays of light. These creatures endure death so much better than people, to quote Mother when she was at her most anxious.

Friedrich – "Fritz" – Carl Gustav Dörries died on February 21, 1953, aged 101.

Henry Gustav Dörries continued life as an explorer, ran a taxidermy store in Stellingen, settled (more or less) in Vladivostok, and died abruptly of potassium cyanide poisoning in 1904. He never married.

Edmund David Dörries worked as a taxidermist at Umlauffsches Museum until his death in 1958.

A fourth brother, Heinrich Friedrich Wilhelm Daniel Dörries, known as Willy, was *Rittmeister* at the English School in Hamburg and lived in the city his entire life. It was said that he, together with his seven sisters, were a comfort to their mother in the decades the rest of his brothers were away on their travels.

Overview of the natural objects collected in eastern Siberia

According to Dr Otto Staudinger the number of butterflies comes to 996 species, of which we discovered 275
    Total: 61,500 specimens

According to my log, the number of beetles ran to 1,490 species, including the smallest (bark beetles, leaf beetles and earth beetles)
    Total: 14,500 specimens

Flies, bees, wasps and other hymenopterans amount to approx. 195 species
    Total: 4,500 specimens

Reptiles, snakes, frogs and salamanders: 448 specimens
Land, swamp and water snails; 340 specimens
Plants in herbaria: 539 specimens
Larvae prepared: 265 specimens
Predators prepared: 520 specimens
Birds: 225 species, 4,805 specimens
122 bird nests complete with 610 egg specimens

Objects were collected from the following tribes: Kyrgyz, Tatar, Bashkir, Ostyak, Buryat, Bira Tungus, Oroch and Killan Goldes by the Amur, the Gilyaks at the mouth of the River Amur, the Ainu on Sakhalin, Chukchi and Koryaks from the Bering Strait, Hyrsin Golds and the Oroch by the Ussuri and its tributaries, in addition to a collection from Korea.

Total number of objects: 8,600

Siberian deer antlers transported to Europe: 1,325

Afterword

Randi Carelius Krogsveen approached me in 2006 with a manuscript written by her great-grandfather, Fritz Dörries. It was a memoir that the ninety-year-old Dörries had produced three copies of in Hamburg in 1942 – in other words, in the middle of the Second World War – in order to give his three daughters an insight into his adventures as a butterfly collector, researcher, hunter and explorer in eastern Siberia, between 1877 and 1899, when there were still *terrae incognitae* on maps of the world.

Three identical manuscripts, approximately 190 pages long, passed down through the family, one of which Dörries' daughter Thecla brought with her when she moved to Norway. Naturally, Randi was interested in her great-grandfather's life and work and wondered if we could help her.

I was willing, of course, but soon discovered I was unable to read what the old man had written. Dörries employed Sütterlin, a gothic form of handwriting discontinued in German schools in the interwar years. But I showed it to my wife, Anneliese Pitz, who had learned Sütterlin from her grandparents in childhood and was able to transcribe the work. We later translated it into Norwegian, so Randi and her family could finally read their great-grandfather's recollections.

The patently exotic and, in many cases, shocking contents aroused Randi's interest as well as our own. Annelise and I decided to travel in Siberia, first on the Trans-Siberian Railway, then on different cruises, on the River Lena and Lake Baikal among others. We began to read up on Siberia – historical and anthropological studies, as well as what fiction we came across. We also forged many relationships in the region. We could not shake off Siberia. It had got under our skin.

In the summer of 2017, we met up with Randi again. She could not reconcile herself to her great-grandfather's spectacular story remaining unknown to the world at large – this was, after all, exciting and important material, especially now, with such intense general interest in nature, above all unspoiled nature; the contrasts between Dörries' time and ours are tremendous.

In an article published in *Die Heimat* in October 1969, the entomologist Herbert Weidner makes a decent attempt to obtain an overview of Dörries' work. Weidner draws on twenty-four different sources, including scientific articles published by Dörries himself, interviews he gave to newspapers and periodicals, as well as eighteen other written sources, authored in the main by Dörries' peers. Weidner also refers to several (unspecified) oral sources, Dörries' surviving family members for the most part, but apologises on several occasions for inconsistencies and the lack of an overview, before he concludes:

The Dörries brothers were among those men who, equipped with vast professional knowledge, outstanding powers of observation, and dogged perseverance, defied every difficulty in order to provide essential material for science, fundamental to the development of knowledge about fauna and flora in the regions in question, as well as in the nascent understanding of the interactions between animals and geography. Unfortunately, these men are often soon forgotten, as the materials they collected are divided among several institutions, and because they themselves have left behind little if any literary trace.

The Russian biologist, E.V. Novomodny also regrets that such men of note should be forgotten. Many years in his role at the museum in Khabarovsk made him fully aware of the importance of Dörries' work, and as he writes in 2012:

> It is beyond question that none of them (Graeser, Dieckmann, Lühdorf etc.) can compare with Fritz Dörries regarding the duration of time spent in our region (22 years, from 1877 to 1899) and the scope of materials collected.

These comments galvanised us.

We set about organising the material, finding many new sources, both Dörries' own and external, interviews and articles, from German, English and Russian publications, and started assembling a structure, a preparatory labour that became both extensive and demanding.

Dörries' hand-written documents are not just ad-hoc recollections, but the memoirs of a very old man. He repeats himself, loses the thread and often mixes up the chronology – events from one expedition are conflated with others that must have taken place during another – and leaves behind several unanswered questions and gaps in his story.

To reach a version as readable and thorough as possible, we had to be rigorous both in terms of content and narrative style – while endeavoring to make our account as truthful and authoritative as possible.

For example, some gaps have been filled with information left by Dörries in other documents – especially in professional articles, letters and interviews. But we have also used some oral sources – for instance the story of the loss of the dog prior to the departure from Vladivostok is a story that is still told in the family. The same is true for two of the anecdotes concerning Wanka.

The story of the linden tree hails back to one single written note, as does the hunting trip with the Goldes, where one of the young tribesmen is found dead the next morning in his hut.

The report about the Daurian jackdaw in Chapter 15 is from a thirty-page ornithological log that Dörries recorded at the request of a certain Dr Bolau at the Naturhistorisches Museum in Hamburg.

Dörries himself did not know how many metres in height the brothers traversed during the mad journey by boat down the River Shilka. At times, he both under- and overestimated the distances he travelled; an oddity in this regard is that he roughly halves the stretch he made on sled from Pavlovar to Vladivostok.

We have also taken the liberty of supplying the text with a few scraps of information about some of the indigenous peoples he describes, and have in places given the names of places, persons, colours and seasons where these have either been left out in a confusing way, or mixed up, possibly due to the ravages of time or because Dörries presupposed the same level of knowledge from his reader as he himself possessed.

Of particular interest may be the visit the brothers make to the katorga on the prisoners' island of Sakhalin, where they without doubt fell victim to a Potemkim village-style hoax. Anton Chekhov visited the island at around the same time and gives, in *A Journey to Sakhalin*, a shocking account of conditions which the brothers Dörries in no way noticed; it seems as if they wanted to think as highly as possible of their Russian hosts, in addition to being more interested in the nature than the culture they found on the island. But here we have of course kept the brothers' naïve perspective, supplying only some dry facts on nature and the names of people and buildings. Contemporary photographs of the facility exist.

When it comes to Dörries' travels through Japan, we have added a few sentences about the historical background for the rebellion that he witnessed.

Finally – Dörries could not, of course, have known that the descendants of the deer populations he brought from the Vitim Plateau live and thrive to this day in Bedford Park, England.

There is no doubt that Fritz Dörries loved Siberia. And we, over the course of the last ten or fifteen years, have developed our perceptions of this strange land. No historian or author worth his or her salt would seek to embellish Siberia's dramatic history – consider for example Chekhov on Sakhalin and Bobby Bobrick's *East of the Sun*. And that is not our intention. But the land could certainly use a different voice. Fritz Dörries *is* a different voice. If Siberia is deserving of it remains to be seen. In our opinion, Fritz Dörries is certainly deserving of remembrance.

Acknowledgements

We are deeply indebted to the following individuals and institutions:

First and foremost, Randi Carelius Krogsveen and her family, for not only allowing us to use Fritz Dörries' memoir but also for making freely available the other material he left behind: letters, articles, photographs, and not least, drawings. Randi has also been an invaluable oral source. Thank you also to Bente Carelius Julo and family.

The staff at the Norwegian embassy in Moscow, for their very kind assistance in procuring Kropotkin's map.

Former ambassador to Russia, Øyvind Nordsletten, for his enthusiasm and practical advice, and not least for his inexhaustible knowledge of Russian culture and history.

Dr Martin Husemann, Abteilungsleiter Entomologie, Centrum für Naturkunde, Universität Hamburg, for guiding us in our search for Dörries in the archives and scanning and passing on the illustrations of butterflies.

E.V. Novomodny, entomologist and biologist at the Museum in Khabarovsk, author of several articles on the activity of collectors and researchers in Eastern Russia.

Leif Aarvik, entomologist at the Natural History Museum in Oslo, for reading through those parts of the book concerning butterflies. He deserves due praise for bringing order to our entomological mess.

Geographer Kseniya Klyuchnikova – our indefatigable friend in Irkutsk, who, for a whole winter, kept us continually updated regarding ice conditions on Lake Baikal, and provided countless relevant source references.

Finally, a huge thank you to Anne Sverdrup-Thygeson, for reading the entire work and providing important advice and clarification.

FRITZ DÖRRIES (1852–1953) and his brothers spent more than two decades in Eastern Siberia in the mid-1800s, cataloging birds, insects and mammals and sending specimens to European museums. Several species have been named after them, including a woodpecker and a deer.

ROY JACOBSEN is one of Norway's most internationally renowned writers. His novel *The Unseen*, a phenomenal bestseller in his own country, was shortlisted for the Booker International Prize in 2017.

ANNELIESE PITZ came to Norway from Belgium in 1974. She has a PhD in linguistics from the University of Trondheim and has been teaching for twenty-four years at Oslo University.

SEÁN KINSELLA has translated or co-translated over twenty books by, amongst others, Åsne Seierstad, Jo Nesbø, and Karl Ove Knausgård.